ORTHO'S All About

Shrubs
and Hedges

Written by Penelope O'Sullivan

Meredith® Books
Des Moines, Iowa

Ortho® Books
An imprint of Meredith® Books

Ortho's All About Shrubs and Hedges
Editor: Michael McKinley
Art Director: Tom Wegner
Copy Chief: Catherine Hamrick
Copy and Production Editor: Terri Fredrickson
Contributing Editors: James A. Baggett,
 Leona Holdsworth Openshaw
Technical Consultants: Michael A. Dirr, Harrison L. Flint
Contributing Copy Editors: Cynthia S. Howell, Ed Malles
Contributing Proofreaders: Kathy Eastman, Steve Hallam,
 Margaret Smith
Contributing Technical Researchers: Cynthia Haynes,
 Carolyn S. Magnani
Contributing Illustrator: Mike Eagleton
Contributing Map Illustrator: Jana Fothergill
Contributing Prop/Photo Stylists: Mary E. Klingaman,
 Diane Munkel, Pamela K. Peirce
Indexer: Donald Glassman
Electronic Production Coordinator: Paula Forest
Editorial and Design Assistants: Kathleen Stevens,
 Karen Schirm
Production Director: Douglas M. Johnston
Production Manager: Pam Kvitne
Assistant Prepress Manager: Marjorie J. Schenkelberg

**Additional Editorial Contributions from
 Art Rep Services**
Director: Chip Nadeau
Designers: lk Design, Shawn Wallace
Illustrator: Michael Surles

Meredith® Books
Editor in Chief: James D. Blume
Design Director: Matt Strelecki
Managing Editor: Gregory H. Kayko
Executive Ortho Editor: Benjamin W. Allen

Director, Sales & Marketing, Retail: Michael A. Peterson
Director, Sales & Marketing, Special Markets:
 Rita McMullen
Director, Sales & Marketing, Home & Garden Center
 Channel: Ray Wolf
Director, Operations: George A. Susral

Vice President, General Manager: Jamie L. Martin

Meredith Publishing Group
President, Publishing Group: Christopher M. Little
Vice President, Consumer Marketing & Development:
 Hal Oringer

Meredith Corporation
Chairman and Chief Executive Officer: William T. Kerr

Chairman of the Executive Committee: E.T. Meredith III

On the cover: Burning bush (*Euonymus alatus*) is a popular
 shrub for fall foliage color. Photograph by Richard Shiell.

All of us at Ortho® Books are dedicated to providing you
with the information and ideas you need to enhance your
home and garden. We welcome your comments and
suggestions about this book. Write to us at:
 Meredith Corporation
 Ortho Books
 1716 Locust St.
 Des Moines, IA 50309–3023

If you would like more information on other Ortho
products, call 800-225-2883 or visit us at www.ortho.com

Photographers
(Photographers credited may retain copyright ©
 to the listed photographs.)
L= Left, R= Right, C= Center, B= Bottom, T= Top, i= inset
John E. Bryan: 7BL, 54 Row 2-3; **Walter Chandoha:** 5T, 12T, 86 Row
2-3, 91 Row 2-1; **Crandall & Crandall:** 17 Row 5-1, 19 Row 1-3;
R. Todd Davis: 17 Row 1-3, 17 Row 3-4, 18 Row 2-2, 80 Row 1-2,
92TC; **Joseph De Sciose:** 16 Row 1-4; **Alan & Linda Detrick:** 17 Row
1-4, 17 Row 3-3, 20 Row 3-4, 50CL, 50B, 68C, 82 Row 1-1 & 3, 82 Row
2 2-3, 82 Row 3-2 & 4, 84 Row 1-3, 84 Row 3-3; **Michael Dirr:** 45CR;
Thomas E. Eltzroth: 16 Row 3-3, 17 Row 3-1, 19 Row 3-4, 20 Row 1-3,
20 Row 3-1, 60BL, 62BRi, 63TR, 64BL, 66 Row 2-3, 74TL, 85T; **Derek
Fell:** 5B, 14T, 16 Row 3-4, 17 Row 4-1, 18 Row 2-1, 26TR, 48T, 56T &
C, 67 Row 2-3, 69TL & C, 71T & C & CR, 72C, 73T, 77C, 78 Row 1-4,
79 Row 1-4, 82 Row 2-4, 82 Row 3-1, 83 Row 2-1, 83 Row 5-2, 85 BR,
89B & BR, 91 Row 4-4, 92TR; **Charles Marden Fitch:** 16 Row 4-2, 17
Row 1-2, 17 Row 4-4, 19 Row 3-1, 20 Row 3-3, 49TR, 73TR, 75TR, 78
Row 2-3, 82 Row 3-3; **Harrison L. Flint:** 16 Row 2-4, 16 Row 3-2, 17
Row 2-4, 19 Row 4-1, 20 Row 3-2, 45T, 45BR, 47B, 51B, 54 Row 2-2,
61CL, 64BR, 65C, 67 Row 1-1, 76CL, 81CR, 84 Row 2-3, 91 Row 2-2;
John Glover: 10BL & BLi, 15CL, 16 Row 5 1-2, 18 Row 5-1, 20 Row 1-
2, 23, 30, 44TR, 45TR, 45C, 49B, 51C, 52B, 60B, 62BL, 63TL, 74BL, 80
Row 1-1, 83 Row 1-1, 83 Row 3-2, 86 Row 3-3; **David Goldberg:** 36CR
& BR, 37, 78 Row 2-1; **Jerry Harpur:** 17 Row 4-2, 19T, 19 Row 4-3,
21TC, 24T, 44BR, 52C, 54 Row 2-1, 71BR, 78 Row 2-4, 81BC, 88 Row
1-3; **Jessie M. Harris:** 17 Row 2-3, 17 Row 4-3, 17 Row 5-2, 20 Row 2-1,
79 Row 2-3; **Lynne Harrison:** 20 Row 4-2, 55CL, 57TL; **Jerry Howard/Positive Images:**
21TRB; **Dency Kane:** 19 Row 1-1, 19 Row 5-1, 20 Row 5-3, 47CR, 74B,
83 Row 4 1-2, 84 Row 2 1-2, 91 Row 1-4, 91 Row 4-2; **Mark Kane:** 16
Row 4-3; **Andrew Lawson:** 6T, 8BR, 16 Row 3-1, 47BR, 48B, 58T & B,
59CR, 69BR, 70CL, 75BLB, 81BR, 87 Row 4-2, 91 Row 4-1; **Kathy
Longinaker:** 36CL; **Janet Loughrey:** 11BL, 16 Row 2-1, 55BR, 60TRT,
78 Row 1-1; **Allan Mandell:** 53C; **Charles Mann:** 24B, 44CL; **Marilyn
McAra:** 78 Row 2-2; **Bryan McCay:** 25BL; **David
McDonald/PhotoGarden:** 16 Row 2-3, 18 Row 4-1, 50T, 57B, 59TR,
60TL, 81C, 85BC, 92 TL; **Michael McKinley:** 8TL, 11BC, 12B, 13T,
15T, 17T, 20 Row 2-4, 22TC, 25C & BC, 26TC, 57C; **Clive Nichols:**
5Bi (Anthony Noel), 14CR (Lakemount, Cork, Eire), 16 Row 2-2, 19
Row 2-1, 19 Row 5-3, 20 Row 4-4, 20 Row 5-4, 47T, 61B; **Maggie Oster:**
91 Row 2-3; **Jerry Pavia:** 10BR, 17 Row 1-1, 17 Row 2-2, 17 Row 5-4,
18 Row 1-2, 18 Row 3-1, 19 Row 5-4, 20 Row 1-1, 21C, 24C, 46TL,
51T, 58C, 66 Row 1-1, 66 Row 2 1-2, 67 Row 1-3, 67 Row 2-2, 72B &
BL, 74 CRR, 75CL & CR, 76BL, 79 Row 2-1, 80 Row 4-2, 82 Row 1-2,
86 Row 1-3, 86 Row 2-1, 86 Row 3-1, 88 Row 1-1, 88 Row 2-3, 89C, 91
Row 5-1, 92BL; **Joanne Pavia:** 56BL, 91 Row 2-4; **Ben Phillips/Positive
Images:** 16 Row 1 1-2, 54 Row 1-4, 61CR, 72TL, 79 Row 1-2, 87 Row 1
1-2, 87 Row 2-1, 89TR; **Cheryl R. Richter:** 17 Row 3-2; **Susan A. Roth:**
11BR, 13B, 16 Row 4-1, 18 Row 3-2, 18 Row 4-2, 19 Row 1-2 & 1-4, 19
Row 2 2 -3, 19 Row 3-2, 19 Row 4-4, 19 Row 5-2, 20 Row 1-4, 20 Row
2 2-3, 20 Row 4-3, 20 Row 5-1, 21TRT, 22TL, 28, 45B, 46T, 46CL,
47TR, 47C, 48TL, 48C, 50C, 51BR, 52TL, 53T, 53BR, 54 Row 1 1-3, 54
Row 2-4, 55T, 57TR, 59B, 60TRTi, 62T & BCi & BR, 64T & C, 65T &
B, 66 Row 1 2-3, 67 Row 1-2, 67 Row 2-1, 68T, 69TR, 70C, 73C, 74
CRL, 76C, 77T & TR, 78 Row 1-2, 79 Row 1-1, 79 Row 2-2, 80 Row 2-
2, 80 Row 3 1-2, 80 Row 4-1, 81TC, 82 Row 2-1, 83 Row 1-2, 84 Row 1-
1, 84 Row 3-1, 88 Row 1-2, 88 Row 2-2, 88 Row 3-1, 91 Row 3 1-2, 91
Row 4-3, 91 Row 5-4, 92BC; **Richard Shiell:** 16 Row 5-3, 19 Row 4-2,
20 Row 5-2, 22TR, 26TL, 27TR, 46B, 49T, 49C, 50BL, 62BC, 64TL,
70T & B, 71B, 72T, 74TR & CL, 75T & BRT & BRB, 76T & B, 77B,
78 Row 1-3, 80 Row 2-1, 84 Row 3-2, 86 Row 1 1-2, 86 Row 2-2, 86
Row 3-2, 87 Row 3 1-2, 87 Row 4-1, 88 Row 3 2-3, 89T, 91 Row 3-4, 91
Row 5 2-3; **Pam Spaulding/Positive Images:** 20TR, 20 Row 4-1, 63BC,
79 Row 2-4, 88 Row 2-1, 91 Row 1-2; **AlbertSquillace
/Positive Images:** 55CR; **Sabina Mueller Sulgrove:** 21TL; **Michael S.
Thompson:** 16 Row 1-3, 16 Row 4-4, 16 Row 5-4, 17 Row 2-1, 18 Row
1-1, 19 Row 2-4, 21Ci(2), 27TR, 32, 46CR, 52TR, 55B, 59T & C, 61T,
63BR, 68TL & CL, 69B, 73CR & B, 79 Row 1-3, 81TR, 82 Row 1-4, 83
Row 2-2, 83 Row 3-1, 83 Row 5-1, 84 Row 1-2, 87 Row 2-2, 91 Row 1-1
& 1-3, 91 Row 3-3; **Mark Turner:** 53B, 60TRB & TRBi; **Kay Wheeler:**
18 Row 5-2

THE RIGHT SHRUB FOR THE PURPOSE 4

THE RIGHT SHRUB FOR THE EFFECT 16

THE RIGHT SHRUB FOR THE PLACE 24

PLANTING AND CARE 32

SHRUB SELECTION AND GROWING GUIDE 44

THE RIGHT SHRUB FOR THE PURPOSE

Shrubs provide seasonal drama. Spring-blooming azaleas and rhododendrons are classic choices for front gardens with stunning effect from the street.

Shrubs alone can make a garden. Without them, you hardly have a garden at all. Shrubs are the garden's backbone, bringing beauty, comfort, and pleasure to the landscape by adding structure to the out-of-doors. Shrubs create a transition from the house to the environment that surrounds it, whether that world consists of eastern forests, midwestern prairies, or western dry lands. Before purchasing another plant for the garden, invest in shrubs. They offer years of low-maintenance satisfaction, often at a minimal price. Shrubs change how you feel about being outside. They can create a sense of privacy and psychological comfort, by hiding unsightly views—and physical comfort by altering wind, light, and noise pollution. Select the proper site and shrub, and nature will keep it healthy and looking good.

WHAT SHRUBS CAN DO FOR YOU

CONTROL WIND: Patterns of wind in the garden can be directed by shrubs. They can create a windbreak to divert harsh winter winds or channel a soft summer breeze.

CREATE SHADE: Light, glare, and reflection levels in the garden are important factors. Create restful shade where there was none, or cut the sun's glare on a patio or deck by the thoughtful placement of shrubs.

SLOW EROSION: For problem areas such as slopes where soil, grass, and flowers wash away, suckering and colonizing shrubs can hold the bank in place.

CONTROL TEMPERATURES: Well-placed shrubs can prevent the hot summer sun from entering the house. The same shrubs may allow winter sunlight to brighten and warm the house, and to lower your heating bill.

MUFFLE NOISE: Shrubs hide the source of street noises, making your time at home and in the garden more peaceful and relaxing.

CREATE PRIVACY: Would you like to get away from neighbors or traffic and find peace in a backyard retreat? Densely branched shrubs form the essence of privacy.

SCREEN VIEWS: Whether your view is the dumpster in the alley or a garish sculpture in your neighbors front yard, you can screen out eyesores with shrubs.

DIRECT TRAFFIC: Shrubs help to direct people and animals where you want them to go, forming either real or perceived barriers to activity.

FOCUS ATTENTION: A shrub with unusual, showy properties can easily become the focus of an entire landscape design.

SHAPE SPACE: Shrubs delineate space. Like walls in a building, they bring a human scale to your environment, creating places for outdoor living.

EASE TRANSITIONS: The shift between constructed and natural environments can be eased by shrubs. They can emphasize or soften the lines of the house to make it stand out from—or blend into—its surrounding environment.

SET MOODS: More than any other garden plant, shrubs can establish the ambience of the landscape. Are hedges formal, clipped, and geometrically placed? Or are they loose and open, delineating meandering paths and boundaries?

ADD DRAMA: Shrubs set the stage. A mass of dark green shrubs accentuates and shows off a sculpture or a colorful bed of flowers.

The flamboyant forsythia combines well with evergreen arborvitae to form an eye-catching and handsome hedge that is also equally effective as a privacy barrier from the street. Groups of intermittently planted shrubs can block sight lines from various angles. Remember to allow openings for access.

OFFER BERRIES: The fruit of many shrubs attracts birds and other wildlife in winter. And some ornamental shrubs (such as blueberry) produce fruit tasty to humans, too.

DECORATE INDOORS: Bring the glory of nature indoors by cutting stems of flowering shrubs and sticking them in a vase. Cut stems of conifers or broad-leaved evergreens for holiday and seasonal decorations.

Purple-leaf Japanese barberry makes a handsome yet thorny barrier to trespass (below). Evergreen boxwood is one of many shrubs easy to grow in containers (inset).

SHRUBS MODIFY THE PHYSICAL ENVIRONMENT

Shrubs can help create a cool, shady retreat that is a world unto itself. In such a place a fragrant shrub, such as this mock orange, is a special pleasure all its own.

Shrubs can make you feel comfortable both indoors and out. In summer, they create cooling shade and welcome relief from the glare of the hot sun. Long, curved plantings of shrubs—set diagonally in the wind's path—can bend the breeze toward you, evaporating perspiration and leaving you cool and content. When winter comes, dense evergreen shrub plantings can protect the inside of the house from icy gusts by breaking them up before they reach the exterior walls.

Erosion, a slow natural process often speeded up by contemporary construction practices, can be tempered by shrubs. The leafy, twiggy top growth and spreading roots of shrubs create a perfect antidote for the pounding rains and ravaging winds that strip away precious topsoil.

A sense of peace, privacy, and tranquility in the home landscape is vitally important. Shrubs can offer this. They can shield you from annoying activity in the surrounding neighborhood. Shrubs with hairy leaves help keep the air clean by capturing airborne dirt and pollen on their surfaces. Shrubs also purify the environment through photosynthesis, a process in which they remove carbon dioxide from the atmosphere in sunlight and restore oxygen to the air.

Large shrubs, such as witch hazel, can arch over a sitting area to block sun and glare.

BLOCKING THE WIND

Shrubs can cool your environment by steering summer breezes your way. They can also reduce air turbulence by filtering the wind through their leaves and branches. An evergreen windbreak planted on the north and west sides of a lot can diffuse the wind's speed, potentially lowering your winter heating bill.

Moreover, shrubs or a dense hedge planted on a wall's windward side can help to reduce turbulence on both sides of the wall. When planting a windbreak, place shrubs beyond the width of the actual space that you want to protect, since wind can travel around the sides of the windbreak.

A shrub hedge can make an effective wind break for a previously uncomfortable area.

HOW TO CONTROL EROSION

Erosion occurs when heavy rains or harsh winds carry away topsoil. This occurs frequently on slopes, which may also be exposed to wind and broiling sun.

To combat soil loss, select shrubs that can be densely planted and that have spreading surface-root systems to hold the soil in place—and dense, twiggy horizontal top growth, rough bark, and profuse needles or leaves to break up wind and rain. Mulch newly planted shrubs to help them get established. Shrubs also are useful where growing and mowing grass are difficult.

HOW TO BUFFER NOISE

The profuse needled leaves of yew (*Taxus*), pine (*Pinus*), spruce (*Picea*), fir (*Abies*), and arborvitae (*Thuja*), along with twiggy shrubs such as evergreen barberry (*Berberis*) and

Prostrate shrubs, such as this bearberry cotoneaster, can be planted on steep slopes to help control erosion.

privet (*Ligustrum*), absorb and deflect sound reasonably well. A mix of deciduous shrubs (those that drop their leaves in winter), evergreen shrubs, and taller trees makes the most effective noise barrier, but foliage must be present from the ground up for a noticable reduction of noise. The best sound barriers also employ a solid wall made of masonry or wood. Although shrubs and narrow plantings by themselves cannot completely control noise, a hedge 6-feet tall can hide the source of noise, creating a psychological improvement. Falling water or the songs of birds can mask unpleasant noise, so the installation of a fountain, a small waterfall, or bird-attracting shrubs can be used to treat noise problems.

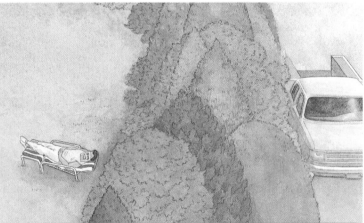

HOW TO DIRECT LIGHT

Depending on their density, height, and placement, shrubs can soften or block glare and reflection. For example, a tall hedge can cool you on a hot afternoon by screening the sun's rays and by reducing the glare from nearby water or pavement. Evergreen shrubs work well for year-round protection from direct or reflected sunlight. In winter, however, you may want warm, cheerful sunshine streaming into the house from the south or east. Deciduous shrubs allow sunlight to penetrate the house in winter and, when leafed out in spring and summer, block direct solar radiation and shade the house.

SHRUBS FOR WINDBREAKS

Barberry (*Berberis*)
Siberian pea shrub
    (*Caragana
    arborescens*)
Escallonia (*Escallonia*)
Burning bush
    (*Euonymus alatus*)
Inkberry (*Ilex glabra*)
Privets (*Ligustrum*)
Mugo pine
    (*Pinus mugo*)
Arrowwood (*Viburnum
    dentatum*)

A mix of deciduous and evergreen shrubs can help reduce the effect of noise.

SHRUBS TO STABILIZE SLOPES

Bearberry
    (*Arctostaphylos
    uva-ursi*)
Carmel creeper
    (*Ceanothus griseus
    var. horizontalis*)
Heather
    (*Calluna vulgaris*)
Cotoneaster
    (*Cotoneaster* spp.)
Prostrate broom
    (*Cytisus decumbens*)
Low junipers
    (*Juniperus* spp.)

HOW TO USE SHRUBS TO SHAPE SPACE

Shrubs that either create or decorate boundaries are an essential aspect of the home landscape. Planted as hedges, shrubs can act as a low living wall or fence, providing privacy or creating divisions between other parts of the garden. Boundaries are an essential part of the modern landscape in both urban and suburban settings.

Space is the basic element of the landscape, and its successful organization is fundamental to creating a usable, liveable, and beautiful place around your home. While the hedges in the front garden shown at left are beautiful in and of themselves, it is the perfectly-proportioned space, or void, in between them that makes this landscape sing. Compare its feeling of open-armed generosity and tranquility to the narrow corridor shown in the garden below, where the confined space makes the eye race to its destination.

Learn to see your landscape as a series of spaces, rather than a collection of objects and plants. Shrubs, of course, are a fundamental tool for shaping the space around you. At their most basic, shrubs can mark boundaries, delineating, for instance, your property lines. Walls of shrubs can enclose the garden into rooms, much as the walls in your home do, with gateways and paths for entrances and connecting corridors. Both short and tall hedges can frame the view, as well as move people and even cars along pathways.

HOW TO INCREASE THE SENSE OF SPACE

The color, size, line, form, texture, and placement of shrubs affect the perception of space in the garden. For example, you can increase perceived space dramatically by forcing the perspective from a single viewpoint. Thus, for a viewer standing at one end of an allée (a landscape term meaning a straight, linear passage), parallel hedges or shrub borders of similar consistent height gradually recede into the distance. To speed up the perceived recession, thereby increasing the sense of distance and depth, slope the tops of the shrubs so that they are taller in the foreground and shorter in the distance. Decreasing the actual width of the passage as it moves into the distance accentuates the forced perspective.

Color is another way to tease the eye into perceiving greater distance. In general, the darker and cooler the colors, the more they appear to recede, whereas bright, warm colors tend to stand out. Therefore, dark bluish-green foliage would retreat into the background when contrasted with leaves of clear yellow-green. Placing shrubs with showy chartreuse foliage at the far end of a hedge or border actually serves to decrease that planting's visual depth.

Likewise, coarse-textured plants dominate fine textures in the landscape. Shrubs of fine to medium-fine texture such as box or privet (that are densely covered with short-stemmed small leaves) make a smooth, neutral statement and work especially well in hedges or backgrounds. Conversely, coarse-textured shrubs with large leaves on long stems accentuate moving patterns of light and dark, thus drawing attention to a planting and reducing the perceived size of the area. Interesting plants with bold sculptural shapes appear closer to the viewer than smooth clipped hedges or uniform shrub plantings that quickly disappear into the background.

Plant size also affects the perception of space. For instance, surrounding a small garden with tall hedges or filling it with jumbo shrubs, flowers, and trees quickly shrinks the space. On the other hand, choosing dwarf shrubs and small flowering trees can lend a little garden a sense of spaciousness, proportion, and proper scale.

1. Screen Out Eyesores:
A shrub border of evergreens makes an effective screen for a neighbor's unsightly play equipment, while a hedge masks a utility area.

2. Create a Sense of Privacy: A living screen can be harmonious addition. Virtually any shrub can be used to create privacy if it is sited appropriately.

3. Enclose Your Spaces:
Use shrubs to create garden "rooms" or surprise elements in the landscape. Block open views for additional interest in the landscape.

4. Direct Movement:
Use a planting of mixed shrubs to not only direct the eye within the garden landscape, but to also direct the flow of foot traffic.

5. Frame a View:
Create an enticing view of the trees, shrubs, or ornament beyond by carefully siting shrubs to make the most of the entire garden.

6. Create corridors:
A mixed hedge of shrubs and perennials flanks a wooden pergola, creating a pleasant pathway between elements in the landscape.

7. Enlarge the Sense of Space: Using shrubs to squeeze space into a corridor increases the sense of expansion in the garden room beyond.

8. Attract Attention:
A specimen may be a single shrub at a visual focal point or in an area where you like to sit and appreciate the plant's color and shape.

THE ROLE OF STYLE

SHRUBS FOR FORMAL HEDGES

Barberry
   (*Berberis*)
Boxwood (*Buxus*)
Holly (*Ilex*)
Privet (*Ligustrum*)
Holly osmanthus
   (*Osmanthus
   heterophyllus*)
Nanking cherry
   (*Prunus tomentosa*)
Rosemary (*Rosmarinus
   officinalis*)
Yew (*Taxus*)
Arborvitae (*Thuja*)
Canada hemlock
   (*Tsuga canadensis*)

Shrubs enclose a traditional garden (below) and punctuate a modern formal landscape (inset).

Creating a garden brings up questions of style. Just as the interior of your home reflects your needs and personality, so the outside of your house reveals similar insights into who you are. For example, does a four-square neo-Georgian home inspire visions of orderly hedges, or would you soften the austere contours of the house with a flowing design based on lush plantings of native shrubs? Both ideas have merit, but they demonstrate different ways of organizing outdoor space. The first style, with its emphasis on symmetry and architecture, is formal. The second, which relies on asymmetrical balance and the plants themselves for effect, is informal or naturalistic.

The style and location of the house influence your ultimate garden style. A suburban center-hall colonial may lend itself to a symmetrical approach highlighting the architectural qualities of the house, whereas a restored farmhouse at the edge of the woods on a rocky hillside brings to mind a more naturalistic setting. Sometimes, the unique character of the site—the spirit of a place—inspires a landscape plan with formal features near the house and more naturalistic elements at a distance.

HOW TO USE GEOMETRY

Formal gardens have a central axis, meaning that the design turns on an imaginary line drawn down the middle of the plan. These gardens are symmetrically balanced so that the layout on one side of the axis mirrors the opposite side. In formal gardens, humans are the master of nature, imposing restraint and order on the growth of plants. Some shrubs become geometrical hedges through shearing or clipping. Others are sculpted into topiary, given shapes of cubes, spheres, spirals, or fanciful animals.

Geometrical surface patterns, which work especially well on flat stretches of land, often pervade the design. Knots—herb or flower beds with a twining design created by low shrubs such as boxwood (*Buxus*) or rosemary (*Rosmarinus officinalis*)—have been part of formal gardens since their birth in Tudor England. Parterres—flat, geometrically patterned beds of flowers and shrubs—originated in the late 1400s but still exist today as formal design elements. Traditionally, knots and parterres were planted close to a

Mix and match to suit your tastes: Contrast formal shrub elements, such as rigidly clipped boxwood, with more natural forms, such as a grove of ginko trees (above) or the open habit of witch hazel (right).

house so their intricate patterns could be appreciated from the upper stories or during after-dinner garden strolls.

If you prefer the clean lines and architectural clarity of a formal design, a naturalistic plan may at first glance seem haphazard and spontaneous. On the other hand, if you are a romantic, the formality of meticulously pruned spherical shrubs on neatly mulched beds is as appetizing as a plate of meatballs minus the spaghetti. Instead, you'd probably relish the long flowing curves, contrasting textures, and variety of natural plant forms typical of the informal garden.

HOW TO USE INFORMALITY

Informal gardens, however, require considerable skill to create. Without forethought, they can end up a chaotic collection of plants. Naturalistic gardens have an asymmetrical balance created by contrasting groups of plants. If you draw a line down the center of a naturalistic plan, both sides are different but carry similar weight and interest. Because this kind of design is not obvious, it is more difficult for gardeners to create than a basic formal design.

The idealized version of nature experienced in naturalistic gardens has a romantic appeal. Human and nature combine as equal design partners, resulting in a greater focus on the plants themselves. Rocks, gnarly trees, and native shrubs add a feeling of rusticity, while uneven ground and winding mulched paths shaded by arching boughs and large plantings of shrubs convey elements of beauty and surprise. Although native plants may predominate in a wild or naturalistic garden, you can also use exotic plants with excellent results. Many woodland gardens, for instance, rely successfully on non-native species of rhododendron and other flowering shrubs for marvelous spring color. The key is finding plants to suit the site in terms of hardiness, soil, and the right amount of water and light.

You may find it advantageous to combine both formal and informal design elements. That's fine—garden design is an accommodating art. If the house lends itself to a formal setting but you like the free-flowing look of a naturalistic garden, you can combine the two with formal elements near the house and casual ones at a distance. A colorful parterre or fragrant knot works well outside French doors, while a tall, informal hedge of native shrubs makes an attractive backyard screen for ugly views and noise.

NATIVE SHRUBS FOR INFORMAL USE

Bottlebrush buckeye
  (*Aesculus parviflora*)
Carolina allspice
  (*Calycanthus floridus*)
Summersweet
  (*Clethra alnifolia*)
Redosier dogwood
  (*Cornus stolonifera*)
Dwarf fothergilla
  (*Fothergilla gardenii*)
Common witch hazel
  (*Hamamelis virginiana*)
Mountain laurel
  (*Kalmia latifolia*)
Mountain andromeda
  (*Pieris floribunda*)
Highbush blueberry
  (*Vaccinium corymbosum*)

Why travel to the woods for a vacation when you can have a natural paradise right in your own backyard? Here are two personal visions of the wild woodland ideal: spring in the Pacific Northwest (left), and fall in the Northeast (above).

USING SHRUBS AT THE FOUNDATION

VERTICAL SHRUB FORMS

Pyramidal/conical
(Taxus cuspidata)

Columnar
(Thuja occidentalis)

Vase/fanshaped
(Hamamelis × intermedia)

Arching/fountain
(Spiraea × vanhouttei)

Oval
(Ilex cornuta)

Shrubs vary in outline. Some have vertical patterns of growth (above) that give these plants an erect, upward-reaching appearance. Vertical shrubs are useful as accents or to punctuate or emphasize a planting composition.

When choosing shrubs for a foundation, try to match the space with the mature size of the shrub, such as these azaleas. If you force a large-growing plant below a window or beside a doorway, you will always be pruning it.

Plant a narrow strip of mixed shrubs and perennials along the foundation of an urban townhouse (below) or apartment building to create the impression of a natural woodland setting.

Foundation plantings appear in front of many American homes. This uniquely American landscape feature started as a cover-up for the tall, lattice-covered foundations constructed under the fashionable front porches of big Victorian abodes. Yet even as the Victorian style passed into history, these voguish plantings started cropping up where foundations were low and there was no need for them.

With careful consideration, you can create an effective foundation planting. Such a planting not only will disguise and lend visual stability to a tall foundation, but also can soften the corners of a house and tie it into the surrounding landscape. Some foundation plantings enhance the style of a house. A symmetrical pattern reinforces the regularity of a foursquare colonial home, while an asymmetrically balanced planting is in keeping with a prairie-style house. A well-designed planting focuses attention on the front door, the focal point of most homes.

SIZE AND PROPORTION The key to a successful foundation planting is a sense of proportion and scale. Large shrubs often look best with a tall house of two or more stories, while smaller shrubs complement the lines of a one-story dwelling.

Pink hydrangea is an excellent choice for foundation planting, creating a transition between house and lawn. Placed away from the house a few feet, the shrubs enclose a walkway and patio for an added sense of privacy.

HORIZONTAL SHRUB FORMS

Rounded/globular
(*Buxus sempervirens*)

Mounding
(*Evergreen azalea, southern indica*)

Prostrate
(*Arctostaphylos uva-ursi*)

Horizontal layered
(*Viburnum plicatum var. tomentosum*)

Weeping
(*Tsuga canadensis pendula*)

Shrubs with horizontal forms (above) pull attention downward, directing the viewer's eye toward the ground and creating a needed transition between beds, borders, foundations, and the abutting lawn or pathway.

Find out the mature size of a shrub before buying it. Choose shrubs not for how they look in the nursery but for their mature size. Too many houses have windows, doors, and front steps darkened by formerly shrub-size conifers grown into giant trees. Try to keep the mature height of doorway plants to about one-third the distance from the ground to the eaves overhanging the walls, and corner plants under two-thirds the distance between the ground and the eaves. Corner plantings are taller because they both frame the house and create a transition to the landscape. If you have an existing, overgrown foundation planting, you may be able to prune the shrubs to fit the scale of the house, or you may have to remove them and start from scratch.

HORIZONTAL AND VERTICAL: Shrubs with horizontal form hold the viewer's attention near the ground or pull the gaze downward. These shrubs create effective visual transitions from the vertical architectural lines of a house into the horizontal lines of open landscape. Horizontal shapes include prostrate (shore juniper, *Juniperus conferta*), mounding (Scotch heather, *Calluna vulgaris*), globose (Helleri Japanese holly, *Ilex crenata* 'Helleri'), bushy (snowberry, *Symphoricarpos albus laevigatus*), and weeping (weeping golden deodar cedar, *Cedrus deodara* 'Aurea Pendula').

EVERGREEN AND DECIDUOUS: When designing a foundation planting, note that broad-leaved evergreens and conifers have a year-round presence, but look best when softened by a few deciduous shrubs. Although you'll want flowering evergreen and deciduous shrubs to create a harmonious effect when they flower concurrently with other plants, don't choose them for flower color alone, because flowers are at best a temporary phenomenon with many shrubs.

LOCATION: Place foundation plants in front of the eaves so they will receive water when it rains and in front of the snow line so they won't be crushed when snow slides off the roof. If your house is limestone or stucco and your plants are acid-loving evergreens such as hollies (*Ilex*) or rhododendrons, acidify the soil; rain may wash the residue of these materials into the ground. Finally, pay attention to safety. Overgrown shrubs near the entry give vandals or burglars an easy place to hide.

The dramatic sculptural effect of many desert natives seems made for display against walls, as shown by this attractive desert foundation planting in the Southwest. The same principle works anywhere, however. There are architecturally striking shrubs for every region.

THE SHRUB BORDER

A spectacular spring border is a wonderful place to contrast shrubs of varying heights and textures. This striking border (above) is a good example of how flowering shrubs such as azaleas (in peach, red, and yellow) and evergreen euonymus 'Emerald 'n' Gold' can be combined to create interest.

The possibilities for enlisting shrubs in beds, borders, and islands are virtually endless. Beds and borders, of course, come in as many shapes and sizes as the plants grown in them. An island bed is an excellent place to display the often spectacular shapes and colors of certain shrubs in dramatic combination.

If you can design a shrub border, you can create a garden. Shrub borders are useful for enclosing space. Not only are they an attractive way to delineate the boundaries of your property, they can turn a yard into a garden by creating privacy and limiting views. Like hedges, shrub borders form the walls of outdoor rooms. These walls can be evergreen, deciduous, or both. They can serve as a background against which flowering annuals and perennials display their charms, or they can make their own brilliant and harmonious color display when in flower.

Shrub borders are more than handsome groups of shrubs. Although a well-designed planting may create a place of visual interest or focal point in a landscape, its plants are too far apart to create the massed, wall-like effect of the shrub border. In shrub borders, mature plants typically overlap by about one-third to create a sense of depth, richness, and mass.

Similarly, a shrub border differs from an island planting. The latter is designed to be seen from all sides. It can be treated as a bold landscape mass with overlapping shrubs or as a balanced but sparser group of plants. The shrub border, on the other hand, will be seen from at most three sides. The back of it is against a fence, wall, or property line.

To create an attractive shrub border, it's necessary to understand how scale, balance, sequence, variety, emphasis, and repetition—the principles of design—affect a border's mass, line, color, and texture—the building blocks of your plan. In fact, making a shrub border is similar to playing with blocks. Some are tall and narrow, giving height and impact to a design. Some are a bit shorter and wider

In a naturalistic setting, evergreen shrubs—such as Rocky Mountain juniper, a ground cover variety of juniper, and bird's nest spruce—can form contrasts that are as striking and beautiful as any to be found in the most painstakingly planned landscape.

A low-growing selection of white-, yellow-, and pink-flowering heathers (left) can create a dramatic tapestry of foliage color, texture, and bright blossoms that also has a long season of interest. By limiting the palette to a single species, the entire setting has a unified theme. Heaths and heathers require a moist, humus-rich, acidic soil, and sunshine.

to create a sense of mass and bulk, while others are little cubes, spheres, and slabs. These small blocks link the main masses of the design and enhance its depth and contrast. Both ends of a well-designed shrub border will have a large shrub or a strong, well-defined group of shrubs that anchor it. In addition to choosing plants for mass, include plants for visual interest. Attractive bark, berries, branching habit, and the color and texture of leaves and flowers give seasonal character and beauty to a planting.

SHRUBS IN THE MIXED BORDER

Mixed borders may contain small trees, shrubs, perennials, and some annuals. Perennials and annuals make excellent space fillers for newly planted, deciduous and evergreen shrub borders where the plants have not yet reached their mature spread. A mixed border offers variety, but requires more care than an all-shrub border, since flower-gardening can be labor intensive.

SHRUBS FOR MASSING

Shrub massing implies using one kind of shrub in each bed or border. In a woodland garden, azaleas, rhododendrons, or mountain laurels (*Kalmia latifolia*) can be grouped under deciduous trees for a stunning effect. Beds made up entirely of roses in a formal garden add elegance and unity to the design, while massing small, fine-textured shrubs such as rosemary (*Rosmarinus officinalis*) or lavender (*Lavandula angustifolia*) adds textural contrast. Before planting flowering shrubs such as azaleas, determine when the plants flower and whether selections with overlapping periods of bloom will create a harmonious look.

GROUND-COVER SHRUBS

Bearberry
(*Arctostaphylos uva-ursi*)
Heather
(*Calluna vulgaris*)
Bearberry cotoneaster
(*Cotoneaster dammeri*)
Wintercreeper
(*Euonymus fortunei*)
Aaron's beard
(*Hypericum calycinum*)
Evergreen candytuft
(*Iberis sempervirens*)
Fragrant sumac
(*Rhus aromatica 'Gro-low'*)
Lowbush blueberry
(*Vaccinium angustifolium*)

THE RIGHT SHRUB FOR THE EFFECT

SHOWY FLOWERS

When you see a shrub in bloom at a nursery or public garden and decide that you must have it, remember that the floral display that attracts you will probably last a month or less. Choose shrubs for their foliage and branching structure, not just for their flowers.

There are several considerations for designing a planting of flowering shrubs. First, try to find shrubs that flower at the same time, creating attractive combinations. Be sure their colors also harmonize with bulbs and other flowers on the property, as well as with the house and other structures. Second, think about which shrubs should be planted in masses or in small groups, rather than individually, for best effect.

Then consider the details of flower size and prominence, fragrance, and the shrub's size and growth habit. Be sure they are compatible in their soil and environmental needs. If your soil is not acidic, keep all ericaceous plants—such as rhododendrons (*Rhododendron*), azaleas (*Rhododendron*), and blueberries (*Vaccinium*)—in an area of soil that can be acidified without having to treat all the soil.

In the chart below you will find examples showing the range of colors possible with flowering shrubs in spring and summer.

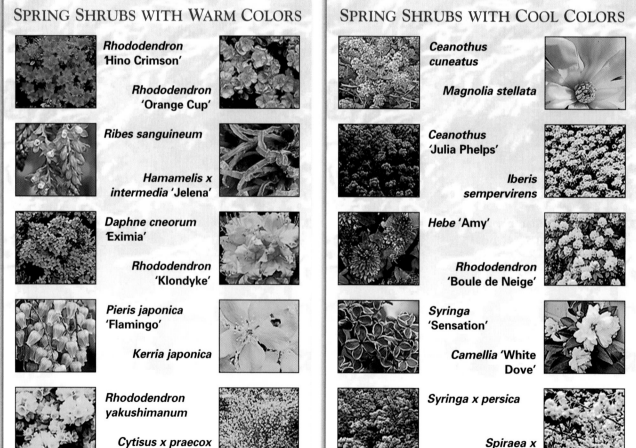

SPRING SHRUBS WITH WARM COLORS

Rhododendron 'Hino Crimson'

Rhododendron 'Orange Cup'

Ribes sanguineum

Hamamelis x intermedia 'Jelena'

Daphne cneorum 'Eximia'

Rhododendron 'Klondyke'

Pieris japonica 'Flamingo'

Kerria japonica

Rhododendron yakushimanum

Cytisus x praecox 'Allgold'

SPRING SHRUBS WITH COOL COLORS

Ceanothus cuneatus

Magnolia stellata

Ceanothus 'Julia Phelps'

Iberis sempervirens

Hebe 'Amy'

Rhododendron 'Boule de Neige'

Syringa 'Sensation'

Camellia 'White Dove'

Syringa x persica

Spiraea x prunifolia 'Plena'

The warm creams and pinks of these spring-blooming rhododendrons and azaleas, cooled by a Persian lilac, are a study in the successful use of complementary colors (left).

SUMMER SHRUBS WITH COOL COLORS

 Rose 'Iceberg'

Hydrangea 'Nikko Blue'

 Calluna vulgaris 'Mair's Variety'

Caryopteris 'Longwood Blue'

 Clerodendrum thomsoniae

Lavandula angustifolia

Hydrangea 'Snow Queen'

Buddleia davidii 'Dartmoor'

Viburnum macrocephalum

Calycanthus floridus

SUMMER SHRUBS WITH WARM COLORS

Rose 'Playboy'

Rose 'Europeana'

Rose 'Abraham Darby'

Kalmia latifolia 'Weston Redbud'

Rose 'Graham Thomas'

Lagerstroemia indica 'Seminole'

Potentilla 'Goldstar'

Hydrangea 'Forever Pink'

Peony 'Age of Gold'

Calluna vulgaris 'J.H. Hamilton'

SHRUBS WITH SHOWY LEAVES

A kaleidescope of complementary shrubs displays the remarkable range of summer-long colors you can find in shrubs with evergreen foliage — including yellow, chartreuse, silvery-green, gray-blue, and emerald.

While seasonal gardens benefit from the careful use of flowering shrubs, it's not the color of the flowers but of the leaves that has the greater impact on the landscape. Leaves are present throughout the growing season and, on evergreen shrubs, year round. By using foliage color to paint the landscape, you can create a long-lasting, harmonious setting for your home.

A leaf color of emerald green has a restful, neutral effect. Likewise, shades of cool blue, gray, and variegated green and white tend to recede visually in the border. Variegated shrubs such as Japanese aucuba (*Aucuba japonicus*) can enliven a shady corner of the garden, the green of the leaves blending the plant into its surroundings while the white reflects the dim light and stands out. The typical yellow-leaved deciduous or evergreen shrub has a golden-greenish tint that can be jarring if overused in the garden but which makes an outstanding highlight in a sunny border. Red, another accent color, is the complement of green on standard color charts. Therefore, a shrub with bright red leaves creates a vibrant contrast against a green background. The exception is a shrub with dark purple leaves, which, from a distance, has a blackish effect on the landscape and creates a dramatic visual hole in a bed or border.

Fall foliage color is as arresting as the color of flowers. It may not last long, but while it does, red, orange, purple, and yellow leaves weave a spectacular tapestry of brilliant color.

BLUE AND GRAY

Pittosporum tob.
'Variegatum'

Cornus stolinifera
'Elegantissima'

Buxus semp.
'Newport Blue'

Euonymus fort.
'Silver Queen'

Juniperus squam.
'Blue Star'

Picea pungens
'Montgomery'

Hebe
'Pewter Dome'

Chamaecyparis
'Dragon Blue'

Picea orientalis
'Procumbens'

Juniperus horiz.
'Blue Rug'

A specimen shrub in an autumn woodland garden will always stand out, whatever the reason for its planting: color, form, shape, or texture. Note the brilliant contrast between the crimson-red shrub foliage, the nearby evergreens, and the golden tree foliage. A specimen shrub should offer a particular presence.

SHRUBS FOR FALL COLOR

Barberry (Berberis)
Beautyberry (Callicarpa)
Blueberry (Vaccinium)
Burning bush (Euonymus alatus)
Cotoneaster
Fothergilla (Fothergilla)
Glossy abelia (Abelia × grandiflora)
Heavenly bamboo (Nandina domestica)
Japanese maple (Acer palmatum)
Oak-leaf hydrangea (Hydrangea quercifolia)
Red chokeberry (Aronia arbutifolia)
Redvein enkianthus
   (Enkianthus campanulatus)
Smoke bush (Cotinus)
Sumac (Rhus)
Viburnum
Virginia sweetspire (Itea virginica)
Witch hazel
   (Hamamelis virginiana)

SHRUBS WITH SHOWY FOLIAGE

RED AND BRONZE

Cotinus coggygria 'Royal Purple'

Pinus sylvestris 'Aurea Nana'

Berberis thunb. 'Bagatelle'

Calluna vulgaris 'Wickwar Flame'

Pieris japonica 'Christmas Cheer'

Osmanthus het. 'Gulftide'

Photinia x fraseri

Berberis thunb. 'Gold Nuggett'

Abelia 'Francis Mason'

Ilex crenata 'Golden Gem'

YELLOW

Aucuba japonica 'Picturata'

Chamaecyparis obt. 'Nana Aurea'

Daphne x burk. 'Carol Mackie'

Juniperus comm. 'Gold Cone'

Spiraea japonica 'Gold Mound'

Chamaecyparis obt. 'Nana Lutea'

Buxus semp. 'Elegantissima'

Thuja orientalis 'Aurea Nana'

Euonymus fort. 'Aureovariegata'

Taxus baccata 'Dovestonii Aurea'

LATE-SEASON EFFECT

Many deciduous shrubs still look terrific after the last fall leaf has dropped. Some bear flashy fruit in red, yellow, orange, purple, or blue that will last until spring. Others carry vibrant berries for hungry birds and visiting wildlife to devour.

Colorful or textured bark also makes an effective winter display in the home landscape. Blueberry (*Vaccinium*) bushes, for example, bear fruit in late summer, while in winter their young stems turn a deep purplish shade of red. Similarly, Japanese kerria (*Kerria japonica*) boasts vivid arching green stems that stand out against winter's palette of whites, browns, and grays in the woodland garden.

Late-season interest is not confined to berries and bark. Harry Lauder's walking stick (*Corylus avellana* 'Contorta'), for example, rises like an expressionist sculpture from the landscape. Here is a shrub with greater impact in winter than in summer, when coarse leaves cover and, to a large extent, hide its curious, twisted branches. What's more, the branches are useful for indoor arrangements.

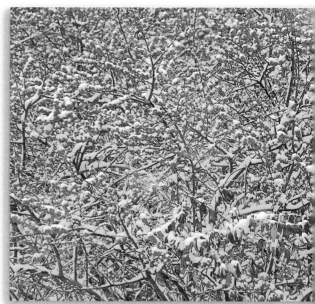

Even deciduous shrubs can offer year-round interest with their attractive bark and fruit. Perhaps the most handsome of all, common winterberry, produces small, showy glistening-red berries that persist in the home landscape throughout the season's chilliest months. Its leaves turn yellow in autumn.

SHRUBS WITH SHOWY FRUIT

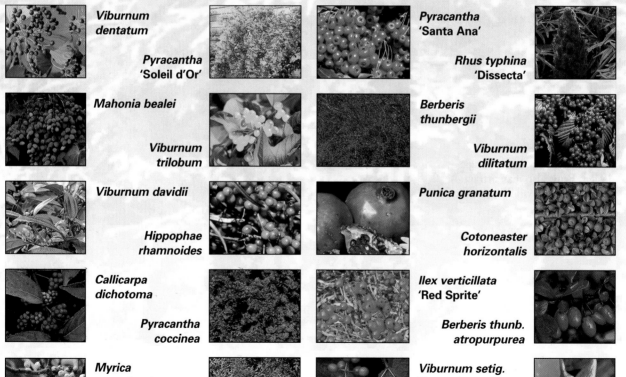

Viburnum dentatum	**Pyracantha 'Santa Ana'**
Pyracantha 'Soleil d'Or'	**Rhus typhina 'Dissecta'**
Mahonia bealei	**Berberis thunbergii**
Viburnum trilobum	**Viburnum dilitatum**
Viburnum davidii	**Punica granatum**
Hippophae rhamnoides	**Cotoneaster horizontalis**
Callicarpa dichotoma	**Ilex verticillata 'Red Sprite'**
Pyracantha coccinea	**Berberis thunb. atropurpurea**
Myrica pensylvanica	**Viburnum setig. 'Aurantiacum'**
Nandina domestica	**Clerodendrum trich. 'Fargesii'**

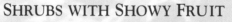

Crape myrtle is a fast-growing, deciduous shrub or tree with attractive winter effect. Multistemmed, it has gorgeous bark, which peels to reveal a mosaic of gray and creamy patches; hybrids can have even more colorful bark.

Beautiful bark characteristics: Red- and yellow-twig shrub dogwoods are grown chiefly for their winter display of bright red and yellow shoots. The colored bark shows better on younger, more vigorous stem growth.

WINTER FLOWERS

Jump-start the growing season by planting shrubs that blossom in winter or by forcing branches of early spring-flowering shrubs indoors. Winter-blooming deciduous shrubs include familiar plants such as witch hazel, (*Hamamelis* × *intermedia*, shown at top) and pussy willow (*Salix caprea*). Among favorite winter-blooming evergreens are common camellia (*Camellia japonica*) and winter daphne (*Daphne odora*).

Shrubs that bloom in early spring are the best for forcing. Forsythia (*Forsythia* × *intermedia* shown above), buttercup winterhazel (*Corylopsis pauciflora*), and lilac (*Syringa vulgaris*), all work well. Forcing time varies, but the nearer it is to a plant's natural flowering time, the faster the stems will bloom. Simply cut the stems up to 3 feet long, then set them in a tall container of clean water until they flower. For quicker forcing, use warm water and set the container in bright, warm, indirect sunlight. Continue to add warm water as necessary. To delay blooming, place the vase in a cooler part of the room and, if necessary, add ice to the water.

SHRUBS WITH EDIBLE FRUIT

Shrubs often produce enticing fruits, some of which are edible and some of which are toxic. Don't sample the flavors in your landscape without knowing with certainty which species produce fruit edible to humans. Fruit may be red, orange, yellow to green, blue, or purple, thus integrating colorfully into your landscape design. Fruit also may attract birds and other wildlife, adding another dimension to the garden. But if you want the fruit for your own table, you may need to cover the shrubs with netting while they ripen. Attractive shrubs with edible fruit include flowering quince (Chaenomeles speciosa), pomegranate (*Punica granatum* 'Wonderful'), beach rose (*Rosa rugosa* 'Frau Dagmar Hartopp'), highbush and lowbush blueberry (*Vaccinium corymbosum* and *V. angustifolium*), and American cranberrybush viburnum (*V. trilobum*).

A blueberry for all seasons: Popular for its edible fruit, the blueberry is a lovely deciduous shrub that starts out in late spring by producing small pink or white flowers (left), followed by edible blue-black berries in summer (center), and finally followed up by handsome leaves flushed wine-red by first frost (right).

SHRUBS FOR YEAR-ROUND EFFECT

Double-file viburnum produces creamy white flowers in spring.

After blooming, double-file viburnum produces red fruits that turn black.

The leaves of double-file viburnum turn a lovely wine red in autumn.

Choosing shrubs for year-round interest guarantees the everchanging beauty of a garden for the longest possible time. Moreover, because top-quality plants can also be expensive, selecting shrubs that are attractive for more than a few weeks a year gives value for your money.

While evergreens offer year-round color and greater consistency, deciduous shrubs change from season to season. Some are noticeable only for a few weeks when in bloom. Others provide months of seasonal interest. For instance, dwarf fothergilla (*Fothergilla gardenii*) produces three seasons of beauty, with charming white bottlebrush flowers in the spring, attractive medium-textured bright green leaves during the growing season, and luminous orange foliage in the fall. Cream-edged tatarian dogwood (*Cornus alba* 'Argenteomarginata') stands out all four seasons with its spring flowers, variegated foliage, and colorful bark (in this case, glowing red stems) after the leaves drop.

Sometimes bark, like dead skin, peels off shrubby stems, giving them a lively three-dimensionality.

Broad-leaved evergreens can have striking flowers and unusual leaves. For example, yak rhododendron (*Rhododendron yakushimanum*) bears white, pink, or rose flowers in May on a shrub covered with leaves that are glossy green on top and felted with heavy brown hair below. The effect of the color and

DECIDUOUS SHRUBS FOR MORE THAN ONE-SEASON EFFECT

American cranberrybush viburnum
  (*Viburnum trilobum*)
Cream-edged Tatarian dogwood
  (*Cornus alba* 'Argenteomarginata')
Doublefile viburnum
  (*Viburnum plicatum* f. *tomentosum* 'Mariesii')Dwarf fothergilla (*Fothergilla gardenii*)
Enkianthus (*Enkianthus* spp.)
Flame azalea (*Rhododendron calendulaceum*)
Harry Lauder's walkingstick
  (*Corylus avellana* 'Contorta')
Highbush blueberry
  (*Vaccinium corymbosum*)
Large fothergilla (*Fothergilla major*)
Lowbush blueberry
  (*Vaccinium angustifolium*)
Oakleaf hydrangea
  (*Hydrangea quercifolia* 'Snow Queen')
Red chokeberry
  (*Aronia arbutifolia* 'Brilliantissima')
Royal azalea
  (*Rhododendron schlippenbachii*)
Seven sons plant (*Heptacodium miconioides*)
Variegated golden twig dogwood
  (*Cornus stolonifera* 'Silver and Gold')
Warminster broom (*Cytisus* × *praecox*)

textural contrasts within each leaf gives this shrub a subtle richness. Oregon grapeholly (*Mahonia aquifolium*) and leatherleaf mahonia (*Mahonia bealei*) add showy berries to the winning combination of yellow flowers and evergreen leaves.

Because conifers add year-round color to the garden, you may be tempted to overuse them. Their density, however, can mire the composition in textural sameness. Especially in foundation plantings, use conifers with rounded forms to bring the gaze back to the earth. Conifers with pyramidal shapes sometimes grow tall and lead the gaze up the walls of the house, emphasizing the disparity between the elements in constructed and natural environments. When designing with conifers, check their mature size before buying. With their wide palette of colors and the proliferation of dwarf and slow-growing varieties, conifers are fundamental to the well-landscaped home.

EVERGREEN SHRUBS FOR MORE THAN ONE-SEASON EFFECT

Common juniper
  (*Juniperus communis* 'Berkshire')
Drooping laucothoë
  (*Leucothoë fontanesiana* 'Girard's Rainbow')
Firethorn (*Pyracantha*)
Gaultheria
Heaths and heathers (*Erica*)
Rocky Mountain juniper
  (*Juniperus scopulorum* 'Table Top Blue')
Sawara cypress
  (*Chamaecyparis pisifera* 'Golden Mop')
Wintergreen cotoneaster (*Cotoneaster conspicuus*)

Aristocratic and evergreen, pines, spruces, and firs are the denizens of the forest primeval and lend an aura of drama to our gardens all year. Nearly all conifers have narrow leaves shaped like needles or flat scales. Most needles stay on the shrubs for three to five years.

THE RIGHT SHRUB FOR THE PLACE

Climate and soil are key factors determining which shrubs will thrive in your region. Choose the right shrubs for your region, grow them with proper soil and light, and you'll save yourself endless trouble. Study the environment and follow its dictates. Altering the surroundings to suit the plants can cause more work in the long run. See what's growing successfully in nearby gardens. Visit garden centers and ask the staff which plants they recommend. Will your shrubs need to survive extreme periods of heat and cold? How much light and water do your potential purchases require? Will the plants you are considering for hedges thrive in the wind, or will they die if used for a windbreak?

Climates across North America vary according to average temperature, extremes of temperature, wind patterns, sunlight and rainfall.

To help you choose the right shrubs, the U.S. Department of Agriculture has published a map of plant hardiness zones, shown here on page 25. These zones refer to the average annual minimum temperatures for each region of the United States. Determine your zone, then look up the range of zones that each plant tolerates in the plant selection guide. Shrubs at either extreme may be borderline in their hardiness, depending upon the planting site and the relative hardiness of the rootstock, seed, or cutting.

Soil also varies from region to region, with differing proportions of clay, sand, and loam. Heavy clay soil lacks air pockets and sticks together when wet. The result is poor drainage or standing water that can suffocate roots. On the other hand, drainage and air spaces in sandy soil are so plentiful that little moisture is retained. Loam, which combines roughly equal amounts of clay, silt, and sand, is ideal for growing many plants. Silt is composed of sediment and rock particles that are bigger than clay particles but smaller than sand. Soils also vary in acidity and alkalinity and in the chemical elements they contain.

By noting the plants that flourish in your locale, your garden can be beautiful, healthy, and worry free.

The Pacific Northwest (west of the Cascades) has warm winters, mild summers, and steady, plentiful rainfall. Similar to parts of Great Britain, the moist, temperate climate makes this area suitable for lavish English-style gardens and a profusion of lush flower and foliage plants, including roses of every kind. Many gardens in this region have a distinctly Asian influence. Note the contrasting colors and textures of the trees and shrubs used in this breathtaking woodland setting without the benefit of blossoms.

The climate of coastal California is similar to that around the Mediterranean Sea. Poor, sandy, gravelly, or rocky soil; wind; salt; glaring sun; and long summer droughts are some of the climatic factors present in this environment. Plants with silvery leaves thrive in these conditions. These plants include favorites such as rock rose (Cistus species), lavender (Lavandula angustifolia), lavender cotton (Santolina chamaecyparissus) and rosemary (Rosmarinus officinalis).

While the western half of the United States tends to have more alkaline soils than the rest of the country, the Southwest has particularly alkaline soil due to low annual rainfall, extremely hot summers, low humidity, and extended periods of drought. Salt buildup in the soil can also be a problem due to irrigation and excessive use of inorganic fertilizers. A xeriscape garden—one designed for low water use—can be as beautiful and colorful as a traditional landscape.

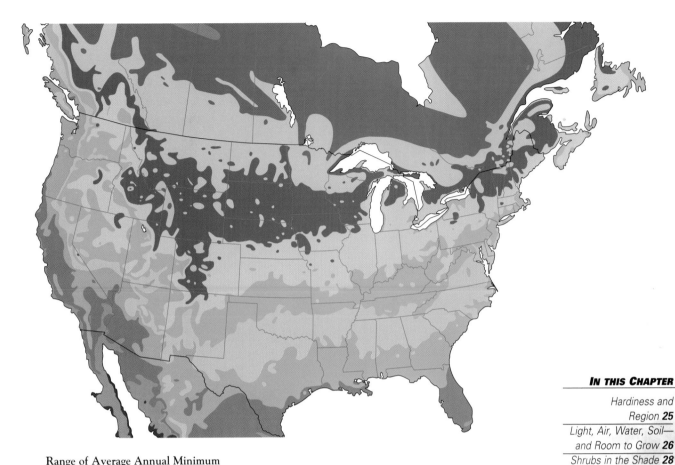

Range of Average Annual Minimum
Temperatures for Each Zone

Zone 1: Below -50° F (below -45.6° C)
Zone 2: -50 to -40° F (-45.5 to -40° C)
Zone 3: -40 to -30° F (-39.9 to -34.5° C)
Zone 4: -30 to -20° F (-34.4 to -28.9° C)
Zone 5: -20 to -10° F (-28.8 to -23.4° C)
Zone 6: -10 to 0° F (-23.3 to -17.8° C)
Zone 7: 0 to 10° F (-17.7 to -12.3° C)
Zone 8: 10 to 20° F (-12.2 to -6.7° C)
Zone 9: 20 to 30° F (-6.6 to -1.2° C)
Zone 10: 30 to 40° F (-1.1 to 4.4° C)
Zone 11: Above 40° F (above 4.5° C)

The Northeast, where woodland predominates, has acid soils. Sunlight is the limiting factor for plant growth, since clouds or precipitation in the form of rain, snow, ice, and fog are present many days of the year. Trees are another factor that limit light. In winter and early spring, sunlight reaches the forest floor, enabling plants to grow. Then, as trees leaf out in spring, old forests grow dim, thus slowing the growth of many plants.

Extreme weather limits plant growth in the Midwest. Summer's heat and high humidity coupled with winter's snow and ice are two aspects of the weather, along with wind that may develop into tornadoes or turn snowstorms into blizzards. Topsoil in the Midwest may be deep and rich, but shrubs have to survive some of the harshest conditions in the country.

The Gulf South has relatively warm winters and hot, humid summers. Rain is abundant, and some southern states may go almost a year without frost. Many tropical shrubs flourish in the South, but plants that require a winter chill to bloom, such as many lilacs, falter under these conditions.

LIGHT, AIR, WATER, SOIL— AND ROOM TO GROW

Thorny, sprawling firethorn is a shrub that's often grown as an espalier and fastened to a fence or wall. It makes a bold statement in hot, south-facing microclimates such as brick walls.

Consider the site carefully before planting a shrub. Japanese aucuba (above left) and oregon grape holly (above right) make excellent choices for shady gardens and for special microclimates such as those found beneath the eaves of a house.

The key to a healthy garden is working with what you've got. Understanding the extreme conditions of your property helps you adapt your garden to the big picture—the climate and geography of the locale. The same factors that affect North American macroclimates also affect the microclimates in your yard. Soil, light, air, space, temperature, and precipitation alter the prevailing climate.

LIGHT

In the garden, the quality as well as the quantity of available light can contribute to microclimates. The house can block the light on part of the property, cooling the site and making it unsuitable for sun-loving plants.

Conversely, a garden bed on the south side of the house with all-day access to sunlight accommodates plants that thrive in warmth and sun. Light reflected from a sunny south-facing wall of the house warms the nearby earth and makes it possible to grow plants that would typically flourish only in warmer climates.

AIR

Adequate air circulation is crucial to disease prevention in colonies of plants. Air pollution may kill some plant varieties, while other, tougher plants flourish wherever you cultivate them. Wind affects the health of shrubs, especially in winter, when icy winds can dry out broad-leaved evergreens or kill susceptible deciduous shrubs in their path.

WATER

Precipitation in the form of rain, snow, mist, fog, and dew is another crucial element. Plants under the eaves of a house or under evergreens or a thickly canopied tree such as a Norway maple must make do with almost no water and sunlight, conditions that

COLD-HARDY SHRUBS

American arborvitae (*Thuja occidentalis*)
American cranberrybush viburnum (*Viburnum trilobum*)
Bayberry (*Myrica pensylvanica*)
Bearberry (*Arctostaphylos uva-ursi*)
Bush cinquefoil (*Potentilla fruticosa*)
Common juniper (*Juniperus communis*)
Creeping juniper (*Juniperus horizontalis*)
Eastern redcedar (*Juniperus virginiana*)
Inkberry (*Ilex glabra*)
Lapland rhododendron (*Rhododendron lapponicum*)
Mugo pine (*Pinus mugo*)
Nanking cherry (*Prunus tomentosa*)
Purpleleaf sand cherry (*Prunus × cistena*)
Redleaf rose (*Rosa rubrifolia*)
Redosier dogwood (*Cornus sericea*)
Rugosa rose (*Rosa rugosa*)
Siberian peashrub (*Caragana arborescens*)
Spruce (*Picea*)
Sweet pepperbush (*Clethra alnifolia*)
Tatarian dogwood (*Cornus alba*)

almost no shrub can tolerate. Tall city buildings can magnify summer heat and keep precipitation from reaching the ground, but privet, barberry, flowering quince, oleander, yucca, and sumac do well under urban conditions.

SOIL

Soil high in organic matter, with lots of space for air and water, is one key to healthy shrubs. Some soils are either too wet or too dry. In either case, you should loosen the soil by mixing in peat moss or compost. Best of all, select plants that tolerate the conditions of your soil.

Soil pH is a measure of acidity, on a scale from 0 to 14. Soil at pH 7.0 is "neutral." Acid soils are below pH 7.0, alkaline soils above. Most plants grow well between pH 5.0 and 7.0, but some, such as blueberries and rhododendrons, grow best between pH 4.5 and 5.5. You can change your soil's pH, but first find out what it is now. Send samples from areas in your yard to your Cooperative Extension Service office for testing. They may analyze your soil's nutritional contents, too.

HEAVY, WET SOIL

Carolina allspice (*Calycanthus floridus*)
European cranberrybush (*Viburnum opulus*)
Inkberry (*Ilex glabra* 'Compacta')
Northern bayberry (*Myrica pensylvanica*)
Red chokeberry (*Aronia arbutifolia*)
Redosier dogwood (*Cornus stolonifera*)
Summersweet (*Clethra alnifolia*)
Tatarian dogwood (*Cornus alba*)
Vernal witch hazel (*Hamamelis vernalis*)
Winterberry (*Ilex verticillata*)

ACID SOIL

Camellia (*Camellia*)
Drooping leucothoë (*Leucothoë fontanesiana*)
Gardenia (*Gardenia jasminoides*)
Heath (*Erica*)
Holly (some, but not all, *Ilex*)
Mexican-orange (*Choisya ternata*)
Mountain laurel (*Kalmia latifolia*)
Redvein enkianthus
 (*Enkianthus campanulatus*)
Rhododendrons and azaleas
 (*Rhododendron*)
Scotch heather (*Calluna vulgaris*)

SALTY SOIL

Bearberry cotoneaster (*Cotoneaster dammeri*)
California lilac (*Ceanothus*)
Manzanita (*Arctostaphylos*)
Rockrose (*Cistus*)
Rosemary (*Rosmarinus officinalis*)
Rose-of-Sharon (*Hibiscus syriacus*)
Rugosa rose (*Rosa rugosa*)
Shore juniper (*Juniperus conferta*)

DRY, SANDY SOIL

Bayberry (*Myrica pensylvanica*)
Bearberry (*Arctostaphylos uva-ursi*)
California lilac (*Ceanothus*)
Silverberry (*Eleagnus*)
Lavender (*Lavandula*)
Oleander (*Nerium oleander*)
Rosemary (*Rosmarinus officinalis*)
Rugosa rose (*Rosa rugosa*)
Shore juniper (*Juniperus conferta*)
Sweet olive (*Osmanthus*)

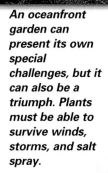

An oceanfront garden can present its own special challenges, but it can also be a triumph. Plants must be able to survive winds, storms, and salt spray.

ALLOW ENOUGH SPACE

Space affects the success of shrubs in the garden. They must be planted far enough apart that the roots don't compete for water and nutrients and that branches don't compete for light. These factors affect the health and growth of your shrubs. Provide room for root growth by planting shrubs well away from wells, septic lines, and fuel tanks. Determine a shrub's mature size before planting, and be sure to select plants that will suit the space without pruning when full grown.

In a foundation planting, choose shrubs that will not grow above the height of the windowsill in order to avoid obstructing light or views. The alternative requires regular pruning in order to reduce the shrub's size and make it fit.

Pay particular attention to the shrubs you plant near the front door. While shrubs on either side of the front door stand out in a traditional foundation planting, you do not want specimens that hinder access to the house or create a security risk by hiding an intruder. Similarly, plants that grow too large for their allotted space can darken your front hall by blocking the door's sidelights. Thorny shrubs are a problem by the front door, because brushing against them may tear clothing (but they increase security when planted beneath easy-access windows).

SHRUBS IN THE SHADE

A shady garden can be a magical place, because shade affects the way we think about space, touching our emotions with its dark, quiet presence. Tall trees arch or buildings loom overhead like the vaults of a medieval cathedral, forming an overstory under which the low-light garden grows. Shade influences temperature, cooling the environment by blocking the sun and providing welcome relief from summer's heat.

The quality of shade varies from light to dense. Gardeners speak of full or dense shade as an area untouched by the sun. Dappled or medium shade filters sunlight through the trees. An area in partial shade has less than 6 hours of sunlight per day. Half shade occurs on the east and west sides of a house. On the east side, a garden will have morning sun and afternoon shade, an ideal situation for many plants. On the west, a garden has morning shade and afternoon sun, which can be intensely hot. To determine the kind of shade you have, note the patterns in your garden at different seasons and times of day.

Foliage color enriches the shady garden. Leaves of dark green, light green, purple, and variegated colors provide muted, all-season contrast. Shrubs with interesting foliage that tolerate shade include cutleaf Japanese maple (*Acer palmatum* var. *dissectum* cultivars),

Japanese aucuba (*Aucuba japonica*), wintercreeper (*Euonymus fortunei*), drooping Leucothoë (*Leucothoë fontanesiana* 'Girard's Rainbow'), and Japanese pittosporum (*Pittosporum tobira*). Variegated plants and plants with white or pastel blooms stand out in dark areas, bringing light and definition to beds. Fragrance is another way that plants touch the senses in a shady garden.

Some shrubs and small trees flourish in both sun and shade. When grown in shady conditions, those plants tend to have fewer flowers and are more delicately branched than the same cultivars grown in sun.

SHADE-TOLERANT SHRUBS

Japanese aucuba (*Aucuba japonica*)
Cherry laurel (*Prunus laurocerasus*)
Chinese holly (*Ilex cornuta*)
Drooping leucothoë (*Leucothoë fontanesiana*)
Gardenia (*Gardenia jasminoides*)
Heavenly bamboo (*Nandina domestica*)
Japanese pittosporum (*Pittosporum tobira*)
Kerria (*Kerria japonica*)
Oakleaf hydrangea (*Hydrangea quercifolia*)
Smooth hydrangea (*Hydrangea arborescens*)
Wintercreeper (*Euonymous fortunei*)

HOW TO USE SHRUBS IN DRY SHADE

Of all kinds of shade, dry shade is the most challenging for the gardener. Typically found under densely canopied trees and under overhangs or next to walls on the north side of a house, dry shade means that plants receive neither light nor water, two elements that they need to survive. Rather than despair, you can deal with dark, barren sites in several ways. You can irrigate the soil, amend it with organic matter, and plant it with shrubs that tolerate dry, shady conditions. When planting shrubs near the house, remember to dig planting holes far enough away from the eaves so rain can reach the plants' roots. Although you can also use drip irrigation to bring them water, they will lack the air circulation they need to remain healthy if planted too close to the building. You can also improve dry shady soil by increasing the soil's ability to retain moisture. Digging in compost, leaf mold, rotted manure, or other organic matter improves the soil's water-holding capability. By selecting shrubs that tolerate dry, shady conditions, however, you'll increase the odds for success. Some

shrubs that adapt to dry shade include Japanese aucuba (*Aucuba japonica*), barberry (*Berberis* spp.), wintercreeper (*Euonymus fortunei* cultivars), common witch hazel (*Hamamelis virginiana*), Arronsbeard St. Johnswort (*Hypericum calycinum*), Hidcote St. Johnswort (*H.* × *patulum* 'Hidcote'), privet (*Ligustrum* spp.), myrtle (*Myrtus communis*), *Osmanthus* spp., Japanese pittosporum (*Pittosporum tobira*), and yew (*taxus* spp.). Many shrubs tolerant of dry shade will grow shorter and thinner and produce fewer flowers and fruit than the same shrubs planted in a sunnier location.

1. North Side:
When gardening in the shade, remember that not all shade is created equal. Open shade occurs on the north side of a building.

2. Half Shade, East Side:
Cool morning sunshine followed by afternoon shade is excellent for many shade-loving plants. Half shade occurs for only part of the day.

3. Half Shade, West Side:
Morning shade followed by afternoon sun may very well be too hot for many shade plants, causing them to wilt in the heat.

4. Dry Shade:
Lack of moisture, not lack of light, often proves to be the culprit when shade-loving plants fail to thrive in their preferred light conditions.

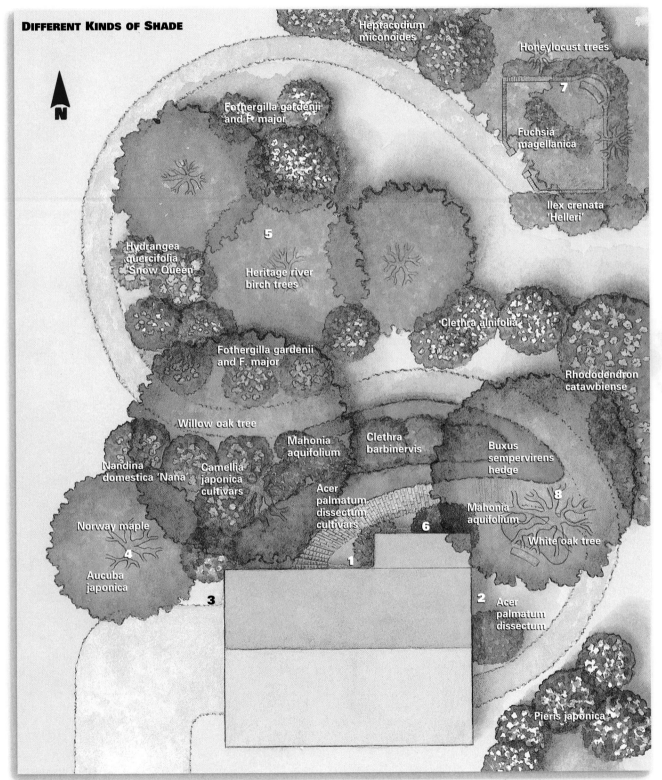

DIFFERENT KINDS OF SHADE

N

Heptacodium miconoides

Honeylocust trees

7

Fuchsia magellanica

Ilex crenata 'Helleri'

Fothergilla gardenii and F. major

5

Hydrangea quercifolia 'Snow Queen'

Heritage river birch trees

Clethra alnifolia

Rhododendron catawbiense

Fothergilla gardenii and F. major

Willow oak tree

Mahonia aquifolium

Clethra barbinervis

Buxus sempervirens hedge

Nandina domestica 'Nana'

Camellia japonica cultivars

Acer palmatum dissectum cultivars

Mahonia aquifolium

8

White oak tree

Norway maple

4

6

Aucuba japonica

1

3

2

Acer palmatum dissectum

Pieris japonica

5. Damp Shade:
Many shaded conditions are cool and damp and can be dressed up from head to toe with a wide array of appropriate plants.

6. Overhang Shade:
An overhanging eave of a house may worsen a difficult location by acting as an umbrella and deflecting rain from the ground beneath.

7. Dappled Shade:
Light shade or filtered shade occurs under a tree canopy of open-branched trees where spots of sunshine filter to the ground in a play of shadows.

8. High Open Shade:
A medium-shade environment occurs under trees that have been limbed up and thinned, such as these oaks.

SMALL-SPACE GARDENS

You don't need much space to have a garden. A corner of soil tucked into pavement in front of a town house, a small courtyard, a tiny lot enclosed by tall wooden fences behind a ground-floor condominium—any of these will do.

Many small-space gardens make excellent outdoor rooms suitable for entertaining. Whether formally or informally arranged, these little gardens depend on organization and planning. Where space is at a premium, prepare a hardscape and planting plan. For a formal town house, you can continue the decorating theme outdoors. A symmetrical design of geometrically shaped beds, neatly pruned topiary in containers, and a low-lying parterre outlined in 12-inch-tall boxwood (*Buxus*) lend formality to a small space.

Planning is just as important for an informal design in the small garden. Using angles or curves, hardscape remains a key element in the plan. For example, brick walls and a brick floor strengthen an asymmetrical arrangement of rectangular or flowing beds, sumptuous with leafy shrubs. Or a narrow, meandering path inside a walled enclosure planted with appropriate shrubs and ground covers could create a woodland effect for the smaller garden.

When landscaping the smaller garden, be aware of the ultimate size of the mature plants. The conifer that looks tidy and compact in its nursery container may one day tower over your garden, shading your entire property (and your neighbor's) and depriving other plants of necessary sunshine. Moreover, large plants have large root systems that compete aggressively with other, smaller plants for soil-borne nutrients.

Instead of buying shrubs on impulse, investigate their mature size before you purchase them. Large shrubs often have dwarf cultivars, often labeled 'Nana' or 'Compacta'. Even these terms can be misleading. *Euonymus alatus*, the popular burning bush, grows 12 to 15 feet tall. The smaller cultivar 'Compactus' grows up to 10 feet high, still too large for many small-space gardens.

Above all else, have fun with the small-space garden. Make sure most of the plants are hard workers, providing more than a single season of interest. Contrasting textures and shapes will enliven the overall design, and, if a bold look is what you want, don't limit the smaller garden to dwarf plants. Large shrubs can be pruned to keep them in scale—or you can simply remove them when they grow too big for the site.

HOW TO USE SHRUBS IN CONTAINERS

One solution to the challenge of a small-space garden is to grow shrubs in containers. That allows you to move them around a patio or courtyard, following the sun or sheltering them from intense winds and downpours. When gardening with potted shrubs, you can change your floral display according to their season of bloom or your changing color schemes.

Shrubs in containers can look as formal or informal as the overall garden style. For example, potted topiaries and rose standards add formality to the garden, while unshaped lavender (*Lavandula angustifolia*), rosemary (*Rosmarinus*), or butterfly bush (*Buddleia davidii*) have a looser look. Planters come in a variety of shapes and sizes, so it's easy to find one that supports the garden's style.

Growing shrubs in containers allows you to push the zone by growing plants intended for warmer climates. With the advent of frost, you can move the container to a sheltered spot for the winter. Because containers sit above the ground, the plants in them are more susceptible to winter damage. If you don't intend to move the container to a protected location, choose plants that are one zone hardier than the area where you live. Move your potted shrubs to a new location gradually. Pay special attention to containers that you're moving from a shaded to a sunny location—leaf burn may result from too much sun too quickly.

The larger the shrub, the larger and stronger the container you'll need. Natural materials indigenous to your locale, including stone, clay, and wood, make attractive containers, especially for naturalistic gardens. Dwarf or slow-growing shrubs make the best candidates for container culture. Large shrubs require more frequent pruning and repotting than slow-growing varieties.

1. Informal or Formal:
A formal garden relies on symmetrical plantings along with elegant touches; an informal garden boasts plenty of curves and color.

2. Small-Scale Plants:
Be sure to choose dwarf, slow-growing, and compact trees and shrubs that won't quickly overgrow the planting area of the small garden.

3. Use Containers:
A container garden blends flower colors, plant shapes, and heights to create the abundant feel of a garden in small spaces.

4. Create a Hedge:
Establish privacy with a row of columnar flowering or evergreen trees and shrubs, or a tall lattice fence and an overhead arbor.

5. Workhorse Plants:
Plant fine-textured shrubs in the background and a few bold-textured shrubs in the foreground to create the illusion of distance.

6. Create an Espalier:
A living fence made from espaliered dwarf apple trees acts as a small-space divider and screen while offering a harvest of fruit.

7. The Outdoor Room:
Eliminate the lawn entirely and install a paved sitting area with a walkway of the same material, which should wind through planting areas.

8. Think Vertically:
Grow vines—and train clambering shrubs—on walls, trellises, and fences or into trees to save space and create the feeling of lushness.

PLANTING AND CARE

Easy-care shrubs can mean more time to actually relax and enjoy the garden. In early May, rhododendron 'Trude Webster' and other spring-blooming shrubs make a handsome yet virtually carefree screen for an escape at the edge of a backyard.

shady Atlanta garden, Myrtle (*Myrtus communis*) for full sun in Sacramento; and Barberry (*Berberis*) for either sun or shade in Minneapolis. Consult the Shrub Selection and Growing Guide (pages 44 to 92) to learn the preferred growing conditions for highly-recommended shrubs. Visit other gardens in your area, both public and private, to directly observe successful solutions. And ask for guidance at local nurseries and garden centers.

Buy only healthy plants. At the local nursery or garden center, study all possible purchases, making sure that tops are well balanced and attractive. Stay away from plants with yellow, dry, wilted leaves or ones with black and white blotches. Yellow leaves may signify a nitrogen deficiency; dry or wilted leaves a lack of water; and splotchy, discolored leaves a variety of fungal diseases. Leaves with holes in them may indicate pest problems. Be sure to inspect shrubs for scratched or damaged bark, another indicator of trouble ahead.

Shrubs are a low-maintenance choice for gardeners. If you buy the right shrubs for the conditions in your garden and help them become well established, they will reward you with years of low-maintenance beauty and vigor. The secret to their health lies in the root system, which spreads deep and wide below ground. These extensive roots allow established shrubs to contact moisture and nourishment beyond their immediate area of growth, where they may have competition from shallow-rooted ornamentals. Growing shrubs is easy, as long as you follow simple guidelines.

CONSIDER CLIMATE AND CONDITIONS

First, match the correct shrub to the conditions in your yard. English boxwood (*Buxus sempervirens*), for example, may be the best choice for a fine-textured hedge in a

CONSIDER THE ROOTS

Check the roots. If shrubs are container grown, look for roots encircling the main stem at the top of the pot. These roots, which can form when a plant grows too big for the container, girdle the trunk and eventually cause its death. Large roots growing out of drainage holes or a split in the plastic pot are warning signs that the plant may have rooted itself at the nursery and could experience shock when moved to a new location.

To help avoid these problems, make sure the size of the plant matches the size of the container. If you see a too-small plant in a large container, it may have recently been transplanted and its roots have not become established. You can check this by feeling the soil. If it's soft and crumbly, it probably hasn't been in the pot long. The soil around shrubs established in their pots should be firm and a little moist. When you must choose between the same-sized shrub in a 1-gallon or 5-gallon size, note that after three years, the 1-gallon sized shrub will be about the same size as the 5-gallon-sized shrub if they'd been planted at the same time. Thus, if you want a new shrub to have an immediate impact on your landscape, choose the 5-gallon pot. If you can wait, however, you can save money and reach the same result with a plant in a 1-gallon pot.

For balled and burlapped plants, ask the nursery staff to unwrap the rootball so you can see whether it has a well developed network of small, fibrous roots. Avoid shrubs with broken, cracked, or dried out rootballs. If the shrub can move up and down in the surrounding soil, its root mass is not well established. Most shrubs sold bare root are roses (*Rosa*), which should be dormant with a moist, fibrous, symmetrical root mass. Do not buy bare-root plants with broken or dried out roots. Remember that the care you take in choosing and nurturing shrubs when they're young pays off later with robust maturity.

HOW TO BUY SHRUBS AT A NURSERY

1. Determine what purpose the shrubs will serve in the landscape and the conditions where they will grow.
2. Buy only healthy shrubs with a balanced, attractive shape.
3. Avoid bark with splits, holes, scratches, cankers, and other damage.
4. Skip plants with parched or wilted leaves and brown to black leaf margins, all indications of drought.
5. Do not buy shrubs with broken branches.
6. Make sure that the roots of shrubs in containers are neither girdled around the base of the plant nor emerging from the drainage holes. Healthy root tips will appear white.
7. Do not buy balled and burlapped plants with dry or broken rootballs.
8. Shrubs should not move up and down in containers or rootballs.
9. Shrubs sold bare root should be dormant when purchased. Roots should look fresh and balanced when the plant is held upright. Do not buy dried or broken bare-root plants.
10. Buy only plants that are clearly labeled.

When buying shrubs in containers, make sure the roots are not girdled around the base of the plant and that they are not emerging from the drainage holes. Make sure the size of the plant matches the size of the container.

Ask the nursery staff to unwrap the rootball so you can inspect it. Make sure it has a well developed network of small, fibrous roots. Avoid shrubs with broken, cracked, or dried out rootballs.

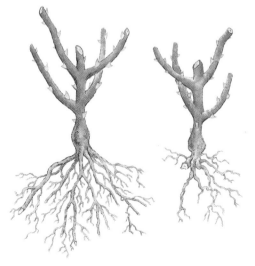

When buying bare-root shrubs, such as roses, be sure the plants are dormant and not pushing new growth. Look for a moist, fibrous, symmetrical root mass. Avoid plants with broken or dried out roots.

PLANTING SHRUBS

DIG THE HOLE: You can plant shrubs at almost any time, as long as you can work the soil with a spade. If possible, however, avoid planting shrubs in late spring right before hot summer weather moves in and in late fall, when shrubs may not have time to establish themselves before the onset of frost. Dig the planting hole twice as wide and slightly shallower than the rootball, because plants often sink as they settle into the earth. The root mass should sit on stable, undisturbed soil. When the hole is deeper than the rootball, it creates a situation that can lead to crown and root rot.

AMEND THE BACKFILL SOIL: Many plants flourish in transition soil or backfill to which amendments such as compost or well rotted manure have been added. Such organic materials help the soil hold moisture and micronutrients. Shrubs planted in amended soil tend to grow better at first than shrubs planted in native soil; however, recent research shows that shrubs often do better in the long run when planted in unamended soil, because their roots spread deeper and wider into the surrounding area. If you decide to amend your backfill, take the soil from the planting hole, estimate its volume, and add either compost or rotted manure. Roughly 25 percent of the final mix should be soil amendment.

REMOVE THE SHRUB FROM THE CONTAINER: Most small shrubs are sold in plastic containers. Before removing the shrub from its pot, dampen the rootball to help it stay intact. A shrub's root system may not recover from a broken or damaged rootball. Invert pot, holding the top of the rootball (this may be a two-person job) and gently tap the edge on a bench or other solid object. A simple shake may suffice, if the plant is not especially pot-bound.

PLACE SHRUB IN HOLE: Inspect the rootball before placing the shrub in the hole. With pruners or a sharp knife, make shallow, vertical cuts along the side of the rootball, cutting any girdled, matted, or tangled roots so that they radiate out from the rootball. Matted roots do not extend into the surrounding soil. Place the shrub in the hole, and work the soil around the rootball with your hands to eliminate air pockets.

FILL HOLE AND BUILD A BASIN: Fill the hole with the backfill to the level of the surrounding soil. Build a shallow basin around the shrub to concentrate irrigation water where it is needed most.

WATER THE SHRUB: Thoroughly water the soil around the root zone. Apply the water slowly so it penetrates the rootball until the soil is loose and muddy. Gently work the soil to eliminate remaining air pockets. Use the basin for watering until some roots have had a chance to expand into the surrounding soil, usually within six weeks. If dry weather conditions require continued irrigation, enlarge the basin as necessary. Be sure to break down the watering basin once the plant is established.

HOW TO PLANT BALLED AND BURLAPPED SHRUBS: Handle the ball carefully, setting it in the hole with the wrap still on. Adjust the height of the rootball as

you would with a shrub from a container. If the burlap has been treated to retard rotting or if the wrap is made of plastic or other nonbiodegradable material, remove it before planting. For burlapped shrubs, untie the material and pull it away from the top of the rootball. Discard the strings if they pull away easily or, if not, let them decompose in the soil. Remove synthetic twine. Cut or fold the wrap back so that it is below the surface of the soil—exposed material wicks water out of the soil. Fill the hole and water the plant in.

HOW TO PLANT BARE-ROOT SHRUBS: Bare-root shrubs, which are planted while dormant, are usually acquired by mail order in the spring. Pruning the bare roots by one-third or more results in a stronger shrub. Store bare-root shrubs in a cool place with their roots in moist sawdust or bark. Soak them in a bucket of water for several hours before planting. Dig a hole large enough to accommodate the full span of the roots. Prune off broken or very long roots and place the plant in the hole with the top root 1 inch below the level of the surrounding soil. Work the backfill soil between the roots with your hands to remove air pockets. Finish filling the hole and water the plant in.

HOW TO PLANT SHRUBS IN CONTAINERS

DRILL HOLES FOR DRAINAGE: Check containers for cleanliness, overall condition, and adequate drainage before putting plants in them. Every container, especially those intended for outdoor use, must drain freely. If drainage is inadequate, water can collect in containers, pooling on the surface and smothering roots. This wetness can lead to crown or root rot and the eventual death of the plants by preventing uptake of oxygen and reducing root activity. Although most terra-cotta and plastic pots have drainage holes, pots made from

other materials may have no drainage at all. The latter can be drilled by first covering the site of the proposed hole with masking tape and then drilling the container at slow speed with a ¼-inch masonry bit.

PREPARE THE SOIL: When possible, use a commercially prepared, lightweight, packaged soil mix. Commercial mixes provide excellent drainage for plants. If you're using garden soil, add soil amendments such as compost, peat moss, leaf mold, or shredded bark, along with perlite to lighten the mix and improve drainage. Typical proportions are 1 part garden soil, 1 part sand or perlite, and 1 part organic material.

Before filling the container with the soil mixture, wet down the soil in a wheelbarrow to make it easier to handle.

PLANT THE SHRUB: Add several inches of soil mix—enough to hold the plant at the desired depth—to the planter, then add the shrub and fill the rest of the container with the mix, leaving 2 to 3 inches between the top of the soil and the rim. This space holds water while it soaks through the soil to the bottom. Pour water on the plant until it runs out the drainage hole to make sure that the plant is thoroughly watered. The water that flows through the drainage hole may contain nutrients from fertilizer applications and from the organic matter in the soil, so use a shallow drainage tray to catch excess water and keep it from staining the deck, porch, or patio. You may wish to add a slow-release fertilizer such as Osmocote.

HOW TO CARE FOR ESTABLISHED SHRUBS

Once established, most shrubs can take care of themselves. Because of their wide-ranging root system, they reach sources of water and soil nutrients far beyond their centers. This does not mean that their needs can be ignored, however. A little attention at the right time will bring more years of beauty and enjoyment.

Provide extra water, fertilizer, and mulch when they are needed. The only time shrubs will need regular watering is during the first few months after planting. Thereafter, water as needed. In the North where the soil freezes, an adequate moisture level before freezing is very important. Slow, thorough, infrequent watering benefits plants more than frequent light watering, which will result in a shallow root system. Even with automatic irrigation, infrequent deep watering is best.

Most good soils have adequate amounts of nutrients. Complete fertilizers supply the three nutrient elements that are needed in the largest amounts: nitrogen (N), which stimulates vegetative growth, but at the expense of flowering in some plants if added in excess; phosphorus (P), which is especially important for root growth after transplanting, and potassium (K), which affects many plant processes. The analysis of a complete fertilizer printed on the container it comes in shows

HOW TO CARE FOR CONTAINER SHRUBS

The gardener's main job when caring for shrubs in containers is providing enough water and nutrients to keep the plants healthy. Unlike plants in the ground, the roots of container shrubs are restricted.

Thus, shrubs in containers need regular watering to keep their leaves from wilting. Give the plant enough water to run out of the drainage holes.

Watering flushes nutrients through soil in a container more quickly than from the soil around plants growing in the ground. Compensate by feeding potted plants a complete fertilizer as frequently as every two weeks in spring and summer or use a slow-release fertilizer. You can also use liquid fertilizer because it is easy to apply.

Water-absorbent silica gel doubles the water-retention capacity of potting soil. This is particularly useful in containers, where as little as a teaspoonful of gel mixed in the soil of a large pot will have significant results.

If your shrub becomes root bound, transplant it to a larger container or shave its roots, compensating for their loss by lightly pruning the top of the plant.

Move potted shrubs gradually from one environment to another to protect them from shock.

Water-absorbent silica gel

Self-watering pot

Drip irrigation systems save water by slowly putting it on the soil near individual plants. They also solve the problem of tall plants blocking the spray from in-ground sprinklers. Shrubs thrive with drip irrigation because they get a steady, slow supply of water and the nutrients that dissolve in water. Drip systems have three main parts: the head, which includes valves and filters near the faucet; the lines, which carry water to plants; and the emitters, which put out water.

A mulch is simply a cover over the soil surface. It can be organic—a biodegradable plant material such as shredded leaves or bark (above), pine needles, manure—or an inorganic material such as plastic sheeting.

how much N, P, and K, in that order, is in the fertilizer. Apply complete fertilizer, following the instructions on the bag, in late autumn in the North, when the shrub is well into the dormant state so there will be time for root uptake before top growth starts in spring.

Mulching shrubs has several benefits. It keeps weeds under control, conserves moisture, and stabilizes soil temperature, making the soil cooler in summer and reducing the heaving that results from alternate freezing and thawing in winter. However, be sure to keep moist mulch well away from stems and trunks to avoid disease.

Organic mulches such as pine needles, oak leaves, shredded pine, hardwood, or cypress bark

CHECKLIST FOR MAINTAINING HEALTHY SHRUBS

- Use pest- and disease-resistant shrubs.
- Mulch shrubs with a layer 2 to 4 inches deep, but avoid piling it heavily around trunks.
- Take daily walks through your garden, looking for changes and potential problems that can be caught early and corrected easily.
- Use clean, sharp tools.
- Weed regularly, especially after rain has softened the soil, when weeds are easily pulled.
- Groom plants by deadheading and removing deadwood.
- Act quickly when pests appear.
- Clean up dead leaves and branches before winter.
- Destroy diseased and infested plant parts promptly.
- Consult your local cooperative extension service office.

work well. Rotted manure or compost feed and condition the soil, but may introduce weeds that will contribute to the weed population.

If you do not have much experience with your soil, it is a good idea to have your garden soil tested. Most laboratories test for acidity (pH), phosphorus (P), and potash (K). A few may test for nitrogen (N) but most do not, because the amount changes with the season.

You can diagnose the nitrogen status of your soil by observing growth and color of your plants. If your plants have good color and are growing well, you probably should not add nitrogen. For help with soil tests and other gardening issues, call your nearest cooperative extension service office.

THE PROPER TOOLS FOR PRUNING

The more you work with shrubs, the more you'll discover the value of good pruning tools. The best tools have steel blades that keep a sharp edge longer and are more comfortable to use than cheaper models. Although high-quality tools are more expensive, the additional cost is worthwhile because the best models have ergonomically designed handles. They fit your hand and protect it from tiring rapidly or from repetitive-motion injuries. It's essential to have hand-held pruning shears that you can use for cutting stems up to ½ inch in diameter. A small folding saw is another useful item for pruning thicker branches. Loppers are long-handled pruners that provide extra leverage for cutting even

stouter branches at the base of deciduous shrubs and thinning young branches on small new trees. Flat hedge shears and electric hedge shears work best for creating a flat wall of foliage.

Note the different blades available for pruners. Scissor-type pruners have sharpened blades that overlap. Anvil-style pruners have a sharpened blade that cuts against a metal anvil. Keep anvil-style pruners sharp, because if the blades are dull, they can crush your shrub's bark. Professional gardeners prefer scissor-style pruners because they give closer, cleaner cuts than anvil pruners. Hold scissor-style pruners with the thin cutting blade next to the main stem for the closest cut.

REASONS TO PRUNE

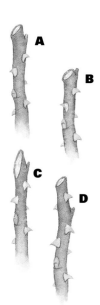

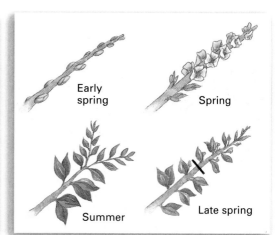

Cut small branches on a 45 degree slant about ¼-inch above a lateral bud that points outward. A) correct cut; B) too close to bud; C) angle too steep; D) too far above bud.

Mature shrubs may need corrective pruning to preserve their health. Corrective pruning may involve cutting away crossed or crowded branches and removing dead, diseased, broken, or pest-infested branches from the shrub. Prune a dead or broken branch immediately. Damaged branches can provide an entry point for insects and pathogens. A balanced crown is also important, because a branch that sticks out of the arc is prone to wind damage and can break under stress.

To stimulate growth and increase flowering, annually remove some older, less productive branches, leaving some mature, flowering stems in place. Prune plants that flower in the spring on old wood at the end of the flowering period. Pruning in fall or winter may remove buds that would flower the next spring. Prune summer-flowering shrubs in late fall or early spring before growth starts. If you wait until growth begins, you'll take off shoots where flowers may develop. Hard pruning of shrubs such as butterfly bush (Buddleia davidii) and some roses sacrifices many smaller blooms for fewer but larger flowers.

Cutting off side branches directs the shrub's energy to the branch tips, pushing branches to grow in the direction they are pointing.

Thinning a shrub removes entire branches back to a main trunk or to the ground, enhancing the shrub's natural form by forcing energy into the remaining branches, which grow more. Prune shrubs with crowded stems by removing the oldest and weakest branches at ground level. Prune the remaining stems back by about one-third.

Shearing, which is used for hedges and topiary, is associated with formal styles. When shearing or clipping a shrub, use hedge clippers or power trimmers to remove its growing points, causing the number of points to increase. For fine-leaved hedges such as yew (Taxus) or boxwood (Buxus), shear by cutting new growth about an inch or two farther out than at the last cutting. This slow growth gives the hedge a constant layer of fresh leaves. Do not use shears for other shrub pruning.

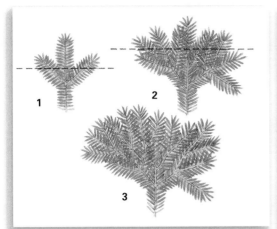

Heading a shrub prunes off most of its growing tips to stimulate lateral growth. Heading forces the shrub's energy from the branch tip to the side buds nearest the tip. The result is a shrub with denser foliage, caused by the plant's growing multiple branches instead of a single branch. Heading forces the dormant buds closest to the pruning cut to grow. Eventually, heading results in a smaller, denser shrub with more branches than one that has been thinned. Shearing is a kind of heading that produces dense growth on the outside of the plant or shrub, and should only be used for formal hedges.

Grooming ericaceous shrubs by deadheading makes them more attractive and stimulates better flowering the following year. Ericaceous shrubs—such as mountain laurel (Kalmia latifolia), rhododendrons, and andromeda (Pieris)—produce blossoms grouped together in trusses. If you don't remove faded flowers, the shrub will set seed. By removing spent flowers, the shrub's energy is available for setting flower buds for the next year.
To deadhead, hold the branch in one hand and snap off the flower head with the other. The same procedure works for lilacs (Syringa vulgaris) and some other shrubs.

Cut off a stem's growing tip to stimulate lateral growth, thus forcing the shrub's energy into producing side branches.

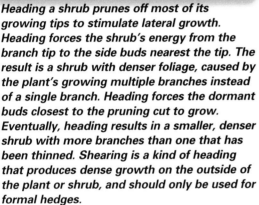

You can rejuvenate some overgrown shrubs or those with weak, misshapen branches by cutting the entire shrub down to a few inches from the ground. This is the fastest way to renew a shrub. Soon, new shoots will arise from basal stems or roots. Choose the strongest and most vigorous stems, thinning out the smallest and weakest. Renew shrubs late in the dormant season before new growth begins. This works well with upright shrubs such as lilacs (Syringa species) and forsythias and with woody, horizontally branched shrubs such as cotoneaster (Cotoneaster species).

Some shrubs are propagated by stem or root cuttings and grown on their own roots while others are grafted. Grafted plants are two plants joined together. A desirable cultivar forms the top growth, while the rootstock is chosen for its vigor. If suckers emerge below the graft union or swelling at the base of the trunk, find where they attach to the understock and then cut them away. If left unchecked, suckers can overgrow the grafted cultivar and produce inferior flowers. Most hybrid tea roses are among the plants that may be grafted onto more vigorous stock.

Pinch off a soft growth tip between your thumb and forefinger just above a set of leaves to encourage branching and, with some ericaceous shrubs, profuse flowering.

PRUNING PROJECTS

How to Batter a Hedge: A formal hedge has batters or sides that slant outward from top to bottom. This tapering allows sunlight to reach all the branches and stimulates new leaf growth, preventing lower branches from dying out. A hedge 5 feet tall could have a base 2½ feet wide and a top 1 foot wide. The easiest method for clipping an established hedge is to use the battered sides visible under the new growth as your guide, but you can also create a simple wedge-shaped template with three pieces of wood to define your chosen form.

How to Make Straight Cuts: Build a wooden guidepost with a short perpendicular piece of wood at the top. Drive the post into the soil next to the hedge. Attach a weighted string or plumb line to the crosspiece. The string should hang a few inches above the ground. Use the vertical line to make straight vertical cuts. For a horizontal guide, site posts at either end. Attach a string between the two posts at the same height and pull taut.

How to Create a Maze: Hedges are the building blocks of mazes and labyrinths. A maze is a puzzle offering travelers a choice of direction. Its paths lead to confusion, dead ends, new directions, and ultimately freedom. A labyrinth, on the other hand, is a single, circuitous path that offers travelers no choices and leads to an end or goal. Both mazes and labyrinths have a spiritual dimension—you lose yourself in a maze and find yourself in a labyrinth. The small maze shown here is simple to understand and to make. It is 30 feet from top to bottom, and 45 feet from side to side, with clipped arborvitae walls 6 feet high and 3 feet wide. Boxwood is also a popular plant for mazes.

HOW TO MAKE AN ESPALIER

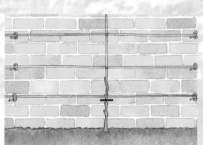

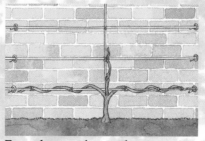

Plant a bare-root, one-year-old whip 6 inches from a wall on which you've fastened horizontal wires 18 inches apart. Head the top of the whip just below the bottom wire.

From the new shoots, choose one to grow vertically and two to grow horizontally. Tie them on. Rub off all other growth and pinch shoots on branches to keep them short.

Head the main stem just below the second wire. Keep two shoots for side branches and one for the trunk. At the top wire, head the trunk, and retain the two side branches.

How to Create a Parterre: A parterre is a flat design made up of colored gravel or short annuals surrounded by low boxwood hedges. Gravel paths connect the sometimes elaborately-shaped beds. A parterre requires regular maintenance. The hedges need to be kept dense and low and the beds and paths need weeding for the effect to work. Keep your parterre in scale with its location. If you have limited time, avoid complex scrollwork in favor of a simpler design like the one shown here. Ideally, you can view it from a terrace or second-story window.

How to Create an Opening: *Cutting a window in a tall, established hedge is a clever way to frame a view and add a new dimension to your garden. First, make a full-sized pattern of your chosen window shape out of plywood, plastic or heavy cardboard. Attach the pattern to a stake. Set it next to the hedge and hammer it into the ground until the pattern is at the desired height. Locate your opening carefully. Remember to stay away from the trunks of your shrubs by siting the window or opening centrally between two plants.*

How to Renovate an Old Hedge: If an old, overgrown hedge comes with your new house, don't despair. Certain hedging shrubs such as yew, honeysuckle, holly, and boxwood can be renovated when too big. To renovate, trim the top to the desired height. Then clip one side of the hedge back to the main stem or stems, cutting the other side to its usual proportions. Wait a year or two until the renovated side shows sufficient regrowth before hard pruning the remaining overgrown side. Prune evergreen shrubs in spring, deciduous shrubs in late winter.

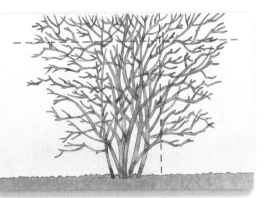

HOW TO MAKE A TOPIARY

To create a cone, pyramid, or obelisk, start with a naturally conical, finely textured, evergreen shrub such as yew (*Taxus*) or boxwood (*Buxus*). For a pyramid, plant the shrub in its permanent location. Head the plant for a couple of growing seasons to make it bushy. In the second or third year, place a pyramidal, wire-mesh former over the shrub, making sure the former is level and upright. During the summer, cut off shoots that grow through the mesh. When the pyramid is full-grown, the mesh will be invisible.

HOW TO TRANSPLANT SHRUBS

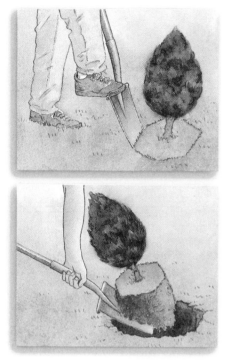

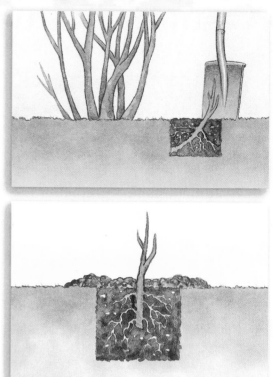

Gardening makes you a participant in an ever-changing and evolving work of art that continues after the initial design and planting. As your garden matures, you may want to transplant some shrubs to new locations. Transplant shrubs during cool, moist weather because roots dry out quickly on warm, windy days. Before transplanting a shrub, be sure to dig a hole in its new location in order to minimize the time that the shrub spends out of the ground. You may want to spray evergreens with an antitranspirant to prevent water loss through the leaves. Move shrubs when they are dormant or relatively inactive.

Before digging a hole, wet the soil until it is moist but not muddy. Dig as large a hole as possible—creating the actual rootball—in order to minimize root loss. Remove any branches destroyed in the process, but do not prune the top after transplanting because

Carefully remove a shrub from the ground, preserving as much of the root system as possible.

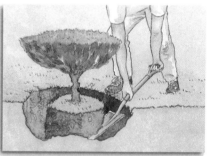

Multiply existing shrubs by transplanting nearby off-shoots. Be sure to remove as much of the root system as possible before planting it anew.

doing so can actually slow root growth. Root loss during the move may cause plants to wilt in the hot sun, unless they have been moved while dormant. Thus, after transplanting large or small shrubs, water them in thoroughly to reduce further moisture loss.

A small tree or shrub can easily be moved to a more desirable location.

First, carefully dig a circle around the shrub to the extent of its branches.

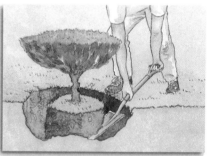

Cut the roots under the shrub, taking care to keep the rootball intact.

Carefully work a sturdy piece of burlap under the rootball.

Tie the rootball up securely and use this to lift the shrub out of the hole.

Use another piece of burlap to transfer the shrub to its new home.

HOW TO RENOVATE SHRUBS

No living part of a landscape is permanent. Plants grow, change, and sometimes die. The dear little cone-shaped spruce you bought in a 1-gallon container now prevents comfortable access to the front door. The Japanese maple has dead branches marring its silhouette, and the rhododendron keeps daylight from entering the front window. The bearberry cotoneaster, a ground cover, has spread beyond the confines of the bed, creating a mess.

When planted below windows or the front door, large evergreens can be hiding places for prowlers. In early spring, transplant the spruce to a site where it can grow undisturbed. Prune the dead branches off the maple. The old rhododendron needs help. Cut the branches near the ground so new ones can grow. Control the cotoneaster by trimming and shaping it. Remove excess cotoneaster plants, moving some to areas requiring more coverage.

Several years later, the renovated landscape is growing well. Helleri hollies give a rhythmic, mounding flow to the foundation, unifying the areas on either side of the door, while the ground cover provides a dark green base. A dwarf conifer stands to the left of the door. The lines of the Japanese maple are now apparent. The rhododendron is denser and more compact, letting light flood the front room.

SHRUB
SELECTION AND
GROWING GUIDE

Foliage can provide color all summer. Below, the variegated leaves of holly osmanthus complement the more ephemeral summer blooms of butterfly bush, spirea, and fuchsia.

Part of the joy of gardening is trying new shrubs. Nursery catalogues are full of gorgeous photographs and enticing descriptions that beckon you to buy. But which shrubs will thrive in your backyard? Throughout this book, we've given you tips on creating a garden specifically for your site.

In our plant selection guide, we give you the facts you need before choosing a shrub. We include a cross section of the best garden plants—classic favorites, promising new and unusual varieties, including species and cultivars that are reliable, widely adapted, and easy to grow. At a glance, you'll be able to name the plant, understand how much cold it can tolerate, and find reasons why that plant is garden-worthy. More detailed information describing the shrub's landscape uses, growth rate, and cultural requirements follows.

Even if you do your research, follow planting directions, and provide appropriate care, not every plant will necessarily flourish. That's okay—change is an inevitable part of the gardening adventure. Exceptionally harsh winter weather or unexpected heat and drought

Rhododendrons, spring heath, and bulbs nestle with dwarf conifers for a showy start to the season.

may kill one plant, while another succumbs to a pest or disease. Before giving up on a shrub, however, check its cultural requirements. Did you plant a shade-loving plant in the sun, or a sand-lover in heavy, wet clay?

Move the plant to a better location and try again. Half the fun of gardening is seeing what does well where and using that information to find plants to buy. Your cooperative extension service or the staff of a local nursery or garden center can also recommend plants that will thrive in your community.

Especially in fall, the drama of changing color is magnified when tempered with evergreens.

ABELIA X GRANDIFLORA

ah-BEE lee-a gran-di-FLO ra

Glossy abelia

6'

6'

- Rounded habit
- Pinkish-white flowers
- Medium-fine texture with lustrous leaves
- Zones 6 to 9

This easy, pest-free 6-foot-tall plant has a graceful, arching silhouette that looks handsome even when not smothered in fragrant, pink-tinged, white flowers from midsummer to midfall. Hybrid origin; species native to Asia.

USE: This hybrid has dense, deep glossy-green summer foliage that turns bronze in fall, making an effective specimen, informal hedge, grouping, or mass, and combining well with broad-leaved evergreens such as *Ilex* and *Pieris*. Growth rate: moderate to fast.

CULTURE: Thrives in well-drained, acid soil with half to full sun and average watering. Experiences winter die back, so prune any dead branches in northern zone 6. New growth comes back quickly.

RECOMMENDED CULTIVARS: 'Prostrata' and 'Sherwood' are lax, twiggy ground covers with smaller leaves. 'Francis Mason' has green leaves with yellow margins.

Glossy abelia can reach 6 feet tall and wide. Above: 'Francis Mason'; inset: typical habit of most cultivars.

ACER PALMATUM DISSECTUM

AY-ser pahl-MAY-tum di-SEK-tum

Cut-leaf Japanese maple

8'

10'

- Refined dwarf tree
- Open habit
- Outstanding fall color
- Zones 5 to 8

No other small tree can match the soft wispy foliage and elegant habit of the cutleaf Japanese maple. Native to Japan, China, and Korea.

USE: Leaves range from greens and purples to unusual variegations. It

has showy fall color, making an outstanding specimen, focal point, bonsai, or understory plant. Plant it with Japanese acuba (*Aucuba japonica*) and leucothoe. Growth rate: slow.

CULTURE: It performs best in moist, well-drained soil high in organic matter and in dappled shade. Protect it from spring frosts and harsh sun and winds. Too much sun or shade can turn purple foliage green and slow the growth rate.

RECOMMENDED CULTIVARS: 'Red Filigree Lace', grows to 6 feet tall with serrated maroon leaves that turn crimson in fall. 'Viridis' is a 12-foot-tall tree with feathery green leaves on arching branches.

Cut-leaf Japanese maple can reach 10 feet tall, but often cascades to form elegant, fine-textured mounds.

AESCULUS PARVIFLORA

ES-kew-lus par-vi-FLOR-a

Bottlebrush buckeye

10'

15'

- Late-season flowers
- Trouble-free foliage
- Suckering habit
- Zones 5 to 8

Give this wide-spreading shrub room to grow and it will reward you with profuse, spectacular, 1-foot-long flower spikes that are white with protuberant red anthers. Leaves start bronze and turn an attractive yellow in autumn. Native

to the woods of the U.S. coastal plains.

USE: Use it as a specimen or for massing and clumping in shady areas, such as under oak, ash, or maple trees. Growth rate: slow to moderate.

CULTURE: Moist, well-drained soil amended with organic matter in sun to heavy shade. Suckering habit (8 to 15 feet) can be troublesome if it's not given room to grow.

RECOMMENDED CULTIVARS AND RELATED SPECIES: 'Rogers' produces flower clusters 18 to 24 inches long. *A. pavia* (red buckeye) has bright red flowers and disease-resistant foliage.

Bottlebrush buckeye forms a thicket up to 10 feet tall. Inset: the flowers of red buckeye (Aesculus pavia).

ARCTOSTAPHYLOS UVA-URSI

ark-toe-STAFF-i-los oo-va ER-si

Bearberry

Bearberry is a creeping evergreen shrub up to 1 foot tall. Inset: Arctostaphylos 'Howard McMinn'.

1' · 5'

- Low, mat-forming ground cover
- Evergreen foliage
- Drought tolerant
- Zones 2 to 7

With drooping, tiny, white to pink bell-shaped flowers followed by bright red berries, bearberry makes a useful, pleasing ground cover for poor, sandy soil. Native to northern Europe, Asia, and North America (south to Virginia, northern Mexico, and northern California).
USE: Cultivate for a slow-growing, fine-textured evergreen ground cover, particularly suitable for the beach. Plant it with *Rosa rugosa* and *Juniperus conferata*. Its lustrous green leaves turn reddish purple to bronze in winter. Growth rate: slow.
CULTURE: Because it tolerates salt, lime, and drought, bearberry is suited for a sunny location at the beach. Set plants from containers or flats 2 feet apart for complete cover in about two seasons.
RECOMMENDED CULTIVARS AND RELATED SPECIES: 'Massachusetts' and 'Vancouver Jade' form handsome mats, and are resistant to disease. 'Point Reyes', from California, is heat and drought tolerant. All have pale pink, urn-shaped flowers and red berries. *A. manzanita* (evergreen manzanita) thrives in coastal California, and has peeling red-brown bark.

ARONIA ARBUTIFOLIA

ah-ROW-nee-a ar-bew-ti-FO-li-a

Red chokeberry

Chokeberry grows 6 to 10 feet tall with white flowers in spring, orange leaves in fall, and red winter berries.

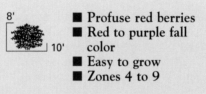
8' · 10'

- Profuse red berries
- Red to purple fall color
- Easy to grow
- Zones 4 to 9

Great for massing, this carefree, leggy, upright shrub offers white spring flowers, great fall color, and gorgeous berries. Native to thickets in bogs, swamps, wet woods, and some dry soil from Nova Scotia to Florida, and west to Michigan, Missouri, and Texas.
USE: Use in large groups at woodland's edge or around sunny ponds to accentuate fruit display and diminish its legginess. Plant it with *Ilex verticillata* and *Clethra alnifolia*. Growth rate: slow.
CULTURE: Grows well in problem wet areas and heavy soil but tolerates prairie drought. Does not do well in dry, shallow alkaline soil. Fruits best in full sun. No pruning is usually necessary.
RECOMMENDED CULTIVARS AND RELATED SPECIES: 'Brilliantissima' (also known as 'Brilliant') has glossy, dark green leaves that turn bright scarlet in autumn, profuse blooms, fuller habit, and bigger berries. *A. melanocarpa* (black chokeberry) has white flowers followed by conspicuous large black berries; wine-red fall color and a vigorous suckering habit.

AUCUBA JAPONICA

a-KEW-ba ja-PON-i-ka

Japanese aucuba

Japanese aucuba forms dense, rounded bushes 6 to 10 feet tall. Shown here: 'Picturata'.

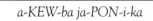
6' · 5'

- Large, leathery, evergreen leaves
- Good container plant
- Adaptable
- Zones 7 to 10

Available in different leaf colors and variegations, this broad-leaved evergreen is a choice plant for dry shade. Native from the Himalayas to Japan.
USE: Does well in dim, north-facing entryways or under densely foliaged trees. *Pittosporum* and ferns are suitable companion plants. Growth rate: slow.
CULTURE: Grows in the shade of buildings, in containers, and under shade trees, where it competes well with tree roots. Selectively cut branches back to a leaf node to keep it dense and rounded and to prevent it from becoming a leggy, open plant. It needs male and female plants to set its attractive red fruit. Variegated forms maintain their color best in open sites.
RECOMMENDED CULTIVARS: 'Mr. Goldstrike', a male, has prominent gold markings on the leaves. 'Picturata' a female, has leaves with a central golden blotch and are yellow-spotted within the margin (it tends to revert to green quite easily). 'Sulphur', a female, has serrated leaves with broad gold edges and a dark green center, which can revert in heavy shade.

BERBERIS THUNBERGII

BER-ber-is thun-BARE-jee-eye

Japanese barberry

6'

8'

- Shearable foliage
- Outstanding fall color
- Red, yellow, and variegated cultivars
- Zones 4 to 8

This upright, arching, rounded shrub has a dense profusion of thorny stems and finely textured foliage. Native to Japan.

USE: It makes a good formal or informal hedge. Plant red-leaved cultivars with pink lilacs, and 'Crimson Pygmy' or 'Aurea' with *Sedum* 'Autumn Joy'. Growth rate: moderate.

CULTURE: Easily transplanted, this drought tolerant, deciduous shrub grows in nearly any soil and in full sun to partial shade. Take care when near this plant, because the thorns collect trash and scratch the unwary.

RECOMMENDED CULTIVARS AND RELATED SPECIES: 'Crimson Pygmy' is a good, red-leaved, ground cover or low hedge up to 2 feet tall and 3 feet wide for hot sunny areas. 'Aurea' has intense yellow leaves that do not burn in the sun. *B.* × *mentorensis* (mentor barberry) is the best for hedging in the East and Midwest.

Japanese barberry is a mound-forming shrub that grows to 6 feet. Above: 'Bagatelle'. Inset: 'Aurea'.

BUDDLEIA DAVIDII

BUD-lee-a dah-VID-ee-eye

Butterfly bush

10'

6'

- Fragrant flowers
- Attracts butterflies
- Coarse textured
- Large flower spikes
- Zones 5 to 9

This sprawling shrub produces flowers in pink, blue, or purple. Native of China.

USE: Treated as a herbaceous perennial, this shrub with arching stems and grey-green leaves makes a delightful addition at the back of the perennial border. Makes an excellent companion to taller plants such as cleome and sunflowers. Growth rate: fast.

CULTURE: Plant this tender shrub in well-drained, fertile soil in full sun. Prune it every year to within a few inches of the ground in the fall after it flowers or in the early spring before growth begins.

RECOMMENDED CULTIVARS AND RELATED SPECIES: 'Black Knight', is a robust dark purple. 'Nanho Blue' is slow, spreading, and mauve-blue. 'Pink Delight' produces huge, fragrant, pink flowers and has silvery leaves. 'Lochinch' has fragrant blue flowers with orange eye and silvery leaves.

Reaching 10 feet tall, butterfly bush produces spikes of fragrant flowers that are attractive to butterflies.

BUXUS SEMPERVIRENS

BUK-sus sem-per-VIR-ens

Common boxwood

4'

4'

- Hedges and topiary
- Dense habit
- Evergreen leaves
- Zones 6 to 10, some cultivars to zone 5

Boxwood hedges are staples of formal gardens. Native to southern Europe, northern Africa, and western Asia.

USE: Hedging, massing, or topiary. Suitable companions include *Pyracantha coccinea* and shrub roses. Growth rate: slow.

CULTURE: To thrive, boxwood needs warm, moist climates without extremes of heat or cold. Plant in well-drained, moist soil amended with organic matter. Mulch heavily. Remove inner dead twigs and fallen leaves in branch crotches to prevent twig canker. Protect it from drying winds and provide partial shade in hot climates. Do not cultivate around this plant's shallow roots.

RECOMMENDED CULTIVARS AND RELATED SPECIES: 'Northern Find' and 'Vardar Valley' are hardy to zone 5. *B. microphylla* (littleleaf boxwood) and *B. koreana* are very hardy. Leaves turn yellow-brown in winter. 'Wintergreen' has superior winter color and is the boxwood most used in the North.

Above: Buxus microphylla 'Wintergreen'. **Inset:** B. sempervirens 'Elegantissima'.

CALLICARPA DICHOTOMA

kal-i-KAR-pa dye-COT-oh-ma

Chinese beautyberry

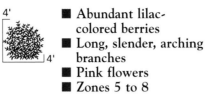

- Abundant lilac-colored berries
- Long, slender, arching branches
- Pink flowers
- Zones 5 to 8

Beautyberry is a showstopper in October, when the conspicuous clusters of small purple fruit are at their peak against a green background of leaves. Flowers are small and clustered. Native to eastern and central China, and to Japan.

USE: Use it massed in the mixed or shrub border, where its fruit contrasts beautifully with shades of green on other plants. Plant it with

The striking fruit of 4-foot-tall beautyberry is produced best in long hot summers when planted in groups.

Viburnum dilitatum and Heuchera 'Palace Purple'. Growth rate: fast.

CULTURE: Plant beautyberry in well-drained, ordinary soil in full sun or dappled shade. Either tip prune to tidy it up or prune it to the ground in late winter.

RECOMMENDED CULTIVARS AND RELATED SPECIES:
Var. albifructus is a white form. The taller-growing C. bodinieri 'Profusion' (Bodiner beautyberry) has 30 to 40 violet fruits per cluster but they are not as persistent as C. dichotoma.

CALLUNA VULGARIS

ka-LOO-na vul-GARE-is

Scotch heather

- Evergreen ground cover
- Fine textured all year
- Mauve to pink late-summer flowers
- Zones 5 to 7

Like a billowing mauve carpet, heather makes a compact, lavish ground cover. Native to Europe and Asia Minor.

USE: In the right conditions, it makes a handsome edging, or plant it in rock gardens. Excellent in combination with Erica carnea, dwarf conifers, and white-stemmed birches. Growth rate: slow.

CULTURE: It thrives in perfectly drained, moisture-retentive, acid,

Reaching 12 inches tall, heather bears stalks of small bell-shaped flowers in red, purple, pink, or white.

sandy or highly organic, infertile soil in full sun. It has fewer flowers in partial shade.

HOW TO GROW: Keep moist, mulch well, and do not cultivate around shallow roots. Prune or shear each autumn after flowering to maintain compactness and encourage heavier blooming.

RECOMMENDED CULTIVARS:
'Blazeaway', 15 inches high, has yellow leaves in spring, green in summer, and orange-red in winter. Mauve flowers appear in late summer. 'County Wicklow', 12 inches high, has green leaves all year, and light pink double flowers from July to October. Many other cultivars are available.

CALYCANTHUS FLORIDUS

kal-i-KAN-thus FLOR-i-dus

Carolina allspice

- Flowers in late spring
- Neat rounded habit
- Easy and adaptable
- Sturdy
- Zones 5 to 9

Allspice produces reddish-brown flowers with spicy fragrance and numerous straplike petals. Native to the southeastern United States woodlands. The dark green leaves—2 to 8 inches long—have a camphor or clovelike scent when crushed.

USE: Plant allspice around outdoor living areas, under windows, beside screen doors, in shrub borders, or wherever its distinctive strawberry scent will be appreciated in summer. Plant it alongside Ligustrum

Carolina allspice can grow to 8 feet tall and is cultivated for its unusual strawberry-scented flowers.

amurense and Rhododendron schlippenbachii. Grow in a mixed shrub border or as specimen plants. Growth rate: slow.

CULTURE: Allspice is a bushy, spreading shrub that grows in nearly any soil but does best in deep, moist loam. It's adaptable to sun or shade but doesn't grow as tall in sun. Pest resistant. Prune after flowering.

RECOMMENDED CULTIVARS AND RELATED SPECIES:
'Athens' has deeply fragrant, greenish-yellow flowers and yellow fall color.

CAMELLIA JAPONICA

ka-MEAL-i-a ja-PON-i-ka

Common camellia

10'
6'

- Flowers December to March
- Evergreen foliage
- Often pyramidal
- Zones 8 to 10

Camellias bear large flowers in shades of white to red against lustrous, dark green leaves. Native to China and Japan.

USE: A fine specimen, it is also excellent in mixed borders and massed in shady gardens. It blends well with other broad-leaved evergreens, such as *Kalmia latifolia* and *Rhododendron*. Growth rate: slow. Can be grown in containers.

CULTURE: Grow in slightly acid soil high in organic matter. Avoid over-fertilization, salt buildup, and cultivation around shallow roots. No pruning is usually needed except to remove deadwood in spring.

RECOMMENDED VARIETIES: 'Debutante' is light pink, double, and early-flowering. 'Governor Mouton' has variegated red and white blossoms, cold-hardy buds. *C. sasanqua* (sasanqua camellia) blooms from autumn to early winter.

Exotic and romantic, camellias grow 6 to 10 feet tall. Inset: 'Debutante'.

CARAGANA ARBORESCENS

kara-GANE-a ar-bo-RES-enz

Siberian peashrub

20'
15'

- Bright yellow flowers in May
- Rapid growing
- A good windbreak
- Zones 2 to 7

Peashrub is extremely hardy with arching branches to the ground. Native to Siberia, Manchuria, and Mongolia.

USE: Plant it with *Arctostaphylos uva-ursi* and *Cornus alba*. Growth rate: medium to fast.

CULTURE: Tough, easy to grow, peashrub tolerates poor soils, drought, and alkalinity. Shear it for denser growth, but peashrub is not suited for formal hedges. Peashrub often is trained as a small tree. It is valued as one of the most adaptable of all plants, even in exposed areas and in all types of soils.

RECOMMENDED CULTIVARS: 'Nana' is a dwarf form with contorted branches. 'Lorbergii' is extremely graceful, with fine-textured foliage. 'Pendula' has weeping branches grafted to a standard. The popular 'Walker', a hybrid of 'Lorbergii' and 'Pendula', combines their fine foliage texture and weeping habit.

While the species can grow 20 feet high, this Caragana arborescens 'Pendula' will not exceed 6 feet.

CARYOPTERIS X CLANDONENSIS

kar-i-OP-ter-is klan-doe-NEN-sis

Bluebeard

3'
4'

- Flowers from mid-August to frost
- Loose, airy habit
- Beautiful against yellow or white flowers
- Zones 5 to 8

Bluebeard is valued for its delicate blue haze of flowers during late summer and early fall and compact size. It is a hybrid. Aromatic foliage.

USE: Bluebeard can be massed in front of sunny borders to emphasize its gray-blue misty effect, or use it as a perennial in the mixed border and with *Coreopsis verticillata* 'Moonbeam' and *Veronica* 'Sunny Border Blue'. Growth rate: fast.

CULTURE: Put bluebeard in good garden soil with average water. Cut to the ground before new growth begins in early spring to keep it compact (2 to 3 feet high) and to increase blossoms.

RECOMMENDED CULTIVARS: 'Azure' and 'Heavenly Blue' produce bright blue blooms. 'Blue Mist' has light blue flowers. 'Longwood Blue' has blue flowers on a gray-green mound of leaves and a long flowering period.

Bluebeard is ideal for late-summer color in a mixed or shrub border. Shown here: 'Ferndown'.

CEANOTHUS SPECIES

see-a-NO thus

California lilac

California lilac can range from open, 20-foot shrubs to low, one-foot sprawlers. Shown here: 'Concha'.

3'
8'

- Best on West Coast
- Fragrant, lilac-like
- Glossy, dark evergreen leaves
- Zones 8 to 10

California lilac is grown in the West for its fragrance and beautiful, fluffy panicles of blue, pink, or white flowers that are reminiscent of the lilac's conelike blooms in miniature. Native to the U.S. West Coast. **USE:** Mass as a ground cover on rocky slopes, or plant as a specimen. Excellent for drought tolerant and native plant gardens. Try it with *Cistus* species and *Artemisia ludoviciana* 'Valerie Finnis'. Growth rate: moderate.

CULTURE: Best in the dry-summer, wet-winter climates of the coastal West. Plant in full sun in well-drained rocky or sandy soil away from sprinklers and sheltered from cold, dry winds. Will not tolerate hot, alkaline soils. Prune only during dry summer months to avoid spreading canker disease. Repeated pruning can shorten its life. **RECOMMENDED CULTIVARS AND RELATED SPECIES:** 'Julia Phelps' produces dark blue flowers on a large evergreen shrub. Carmel creeper (*C. griseus* var. *horizontalis*) develops 2-inch blue flower panicles on 2- to 3-foot-high spreading evergreen shrub with lustrous, glossy green leaves.

CHAENOMELES SPECIOSA

kee-NAH-ma-leez spee-see-OH-sa

Common flowering quince

Flowering quince is a spring-flowering shrub that reaches about 8 feet tall. Inset: 'Nicoline'.

8'
8'

- Early spring flowers
- Thorniness good for barriers
- Fragrant fruit used in jams and jellies
- Zones 5 to 9

This easy-to-grow shrub makes an effective barrier with red, scarlet, pink, or white flowers. Produces edible, aromatic, applelike yellow to green or purplish green fruits. Native to China. **USE:** Use as a hedge or barrier. Grow in a shrub border or on a bank or train against a wall. Combine with bulbs such as *Narcissus* 'February Gold' and *Scilla siberica*. Growth rate: moderate.

CULTURE: Flowering quince likes full sun and is adaptable to many types of soil, including prairie drought. Will thrive against a slightly shaded wall, but performs best—and produces fruit best—in full sun. Prune annually after spring bloom. May be renewed by pruning to 6 inches from the ground after blooming. Tolerant of pollution and urban environments. **RECOMMENDED CULTIVARS AND RELATED SPECIES:** 'Cameo' develops prolific double apricot-colored flowers on a nearly thornless, low-growing shrub. C. × *superba* 'Texas Scarlet' is a compact, spreading shrub with abundant tomato-red blossoms.

CHAMAECYPARIS SPECIES

kam-ee-SIP-a-rus

False cypress

Above: Chamaecyparis pisifera 'Filifera Aurea'. Inset: Chamaecyparis obtusa 'Hinoki'.

3'
4'

- Evergreen foliage
- Small tufts to trees
- Medium texture
- Dwarf cultivars
- Zones 5 to 8, depending on species

Foliage may by bright yellow, deep green, gray, or blue. Some are adapted to moist coastal climates, others the harsher conditions of the Midwest. Native to Japan, Formosa, and the U.S. West Coast. **USE:** False-cypress can be used as a specimen or in a mixed border. Yellow cultivars look good with *Berberis thunbergii* 'Crimson Pygmy'; dark green and blue cultivars go with *B. thunbergii* 'Aurea'. Growth rate: slow for dwarf cultivars.

CULTURE: Give it rich, well-drained soil, full sun in moist, mild climates, and partial shade elsewhere. Transplant it in spring. Protect it from hot, drying winds. **RECOMMENDED CULTIVARS AND RELATED SPECIES:** Sawara cypress (*C. pisifera*) prefers acid soil and loses its inner foliage with age. 'Boulevard' has silver-blue foliage in a compact, heavy-textured cone; it grows 15 feet tall. 'Golden Mop' has bright gold threadlike foliage. Hinoki cypress (*C. obtusa*) tolerates neutral soils and is excellent for the Midwest. Dwarf hinoki cypress 'Nana Gracilis' eventually grows conical, 7 feet high and 3 feet wide. Fernspray cypress 'Filicoides' grows to 10 feet with twisted, orange stems.

CHOISYA TERNATA

CHOY-zya ter-NAH-ta

Mexican orange

8'

10'

■ White flowers
■ Potent fragrance
■ Compact form
■ Zones 8 (southern) to 10

Grow Mexican orange for its white, sweetly scented flowers and its handsome, glossy, dark green evergreen foliage. Native to Mexico.
USE: Plant it for fragrance near entryways, outdoor living areas, windows, walkways, and paths—wherever fragrance can be enjoyed. Great in a shrub border or against a wall. Plant it with *Daphne odora* 'Marginata' and *Lagerstroemia indica*. Growth rate: moderate.
CULTURE: Grow Mexican orange in well-drained, acid soil rich in organic matter, and in full sun at the coast but in partial shade in climates with hot summers. Too much shade makes it leggy and prone to insect attacks. Water infrequently but deeply and prune yearly to maintain a compact form about 4 to 5 feet high and wide.
RECOMMENDED CULTIVAR: 'Sundance' has golden foliage and fragrant white flowers.

Reaching up to 8 feet tall, evergreen Mexican orange produces white, sweetly almond-scented flowers.

CISTUS SPECIES

SIS-tus

Rock rose

3'

4'

■ Fragrant foliage
■ Low-maintenance
■ Five-petaled flowers
■ Gray-green foliage
■ Zones 8 to 10

Evergreen produces white, pink, rosy red, or purple flowers. Native to the Mediterranean.
USE: Rock rose is a colorful, drought-resistant, salt-tolerant, large-scale bank and ground cover that grows as an irregular mound 1 to 6 feet high. Use rock rose with *Leptospermum scoparium* and *Nerium oleander*. Growth rate: moderate.
CULTURE: Rock rose does best on the West Coast in fast-draining soil. Pinch tips of young plants to encourage denser growth. Do not move it once it's established, and avoid hard pruning.
RECOMMENDED CULTIVARS AND RELATED SPECIES: 'Peggy Sammons' has delicate pink blooms and gray-green, downy stems on a mid-size shrub. Laurel rock rose (*C. laurifolius*) is the hardiest species (reaching up to 6 feet in height) with 2- to 3-inch white blossoms with yellow centers and leathery gray-green foliage.

Often short-lived, rock rose grows to about 3 feet. Shown here: 'Peggy Sammons'.

CLERODENDRUM TRICHOTOMUM

clare-oh-DEN-drum try-ko-TO-mum

Harlequin glory bower

15'

20'

■ Tubular flowers
■ Blue berries
■ Vigorous
■ Zones 6 to 9

Very fragrant mid- to late-summer white flowers, enclosed in maroon calyxes, with brilliant blue berries in early autumn make this an excellent addition to the garden. This upright, bushy shrub is native to eastern China and Japan.
USE: Useful in shrub or mixed border for late-season interest. Suitable for the shrub border, glory bower can be trained over a trellis, pergola or other support. Combine it with *Clethra alnifolia* 'Paniculata' and 'Pink Spire'. Growth rate: fast.
CULTURE: Plant harlequin glory bower in moist, well-drained soil in full sun to partial shade. Especially in northern parts of zone 6, treat it like a perennial and cut it back before new growth begins in spring. May become invasive by suckering.
RECOMMENDED RELATED SPECIES: *C. ugandense* bears striking blue to violet flowers.

Ultimately reaching 15 to 20 feet tall, glory bower is valued for its showy late flowers and needs little pruning.

CLETHRA ALNIFOLIA

KLETH-ra all-ni-FOH-li-a

Summersweet

8'
8'

- Fragrant flowers
- Yellow fall color
- Broad, oval habit
- Attracts bees
- Zones 3 to 9

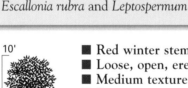

Summersweet grows 8 feet tall and wide with fragrant white late-season flowers, and yellow fall foliage.

Summersweet has medium texture and fragrant white flower spikes in late summer. Native to swamps and moist sandy soils from Maine to Florida.

USE: It can be used in wet, shady areas of the garden but thrives just about anywhere. Perfect for a mixed border or woodland. Summersweet combines well with *Itea virginica* and *Ilex glabra*. Growth rate: slow.

CULTURE: Summersweet grows best in moist, acid soil supplemented with organic matter. Plant in early spring and water profusely. When transplanting into wet soils, ease the transition by planting 3 to 4 inches higher than the soil level and by mulching. Prune after flowering in late summer, allowing the shrub to keep its dense, oval shape.

RECOMMENDED CULTIVARS AND RELATED SPECIES: 'Paniculata' is superior to the species because of its abundant, longer flower spikes. 'Rosea' has pink-tinged white flowers. 'Hummingbird' is a mounded, spreading dwarf good for ground cover. 'Ruby Spice' has deep rose flowers; the color persists.

COPROSMA REPENS

co-PROZ-ma REE-penz

Mirror plant

6'
8'

- Glossy evergreen foliage
- Inconspicuous flowers and fruit
- Upright habit
- Zones 9 to 10

With fast growth to 6 feet in height, mirror plant is valued for its glossy foliage. Shown above: 'Picturata'.

Native to New Zealand, mirror plant (also known as looking-glass plant) is sometimes grown for its orange-red berries in late summer to early autumn. The funnel-shaped flowers are rather insignificant. The most attractive forms are grown for their showy, fleshy foliage.

USE: Hedge, screen, foundation plant, or espalier. Great in the rock garden or shrub border. Use it with *Escallonia rubra* and *Leptospermum scoparium*. Growth rate: fast.

CULTURE: Salt- and drought-tolerant when established, it does well in virtually any soil. Mirror plant needs full sun on the coast and partial shade in hot inland areas. Will survive in areas only with little frost. Prune regularly to keep dense and neat.

RELATED SPECIES: *C. × kirkii* is a widespreading, 2- to 3-foot-high irregular shrub that makes a tough evergreen ground cover, especially where erosion may be a problem. In autumn, it produces oblong berries that are transluscent white, flushed or flecked with red. 'Variegata' has white-margined, gray-green leaves and white berries.

CORNUS ALBA 'SIBIRICA'

KOR-nus AL-ba sigh-BEER-i-ca

Redtwig dogwood

10'
15'

- Red winter stems
- Loose, open, erect
- Medium texture
- Easy to grow
- Zones 3 to 8

Redtwig dogwood grows to 10 feet tall and is great in waterlogged soils. Its winter effect can be outstanding.

Brightly colored stems are an arresting sight in the winter landscape. Native from Siberia to Manchuria and North Korea.

USE: Use it in the shrub border or massed on a large scale along drives, on banks, or naturalized around a pond. Plant it with *C. sericea* 'Flaviramea' and *Myrica pensylvanica*. Growth rate: fast.

CULTURE: Adapts to nearly any soil in sun or light shade. Remove at least one-third of the old growth—more if you want a compact plant—every spring to encourage vigorous new growth with bright red stems.

RECOMMENDED CULTIVARS AND RELATED SPECIES: 'Argenteo-marginata', cream-edged Tatarian dogwood, has leaves with creamy white edges and green centers. Redosier dogwood (*C. stolonifera*) has bright to dark red winter stem color and tolerates water-logged soils. 'Flaviramea' has bright yellow winter stem color but is susceptible to disease. 'Isanti' is a dwarf form. 'Silver and Gold' has yellow stems and leaves with cream-colored margins.

CORYLOPSIS PAUCIFLORA

kor-i-LOP-sis paw-si-FLOR-a

Buttercup winter hazel

5'

8'

- Fragrant flowers
- Fine to medium texture
- Yellow fall color
- Zones 6 to 8

This small shrub is valued for its delicate, soft yellow flowers, fine zigzag twigs, and dainty, horizontally spreading habit. Native to Japan.
USE: Mass it in a woodland setting or against a dark background to show off its lovely spring flowers. Winter hazel looks good with *Juniperus chinensis* 'Robusta Green' and *Rhododendron mucronulatum*. Growth rate: moderate.
CULTURE: Plant buttercup winter hazel in well-drained, moist, somewhat acid soil in partial, dappled, or afternoon shade. If well placed, it requires little care. Renew by pruning off oldest wood after or during bloom.
RELATED SPECIES: Spike winter hazel (*C. spicata*) is hardy to zone 5 and is similar in size to *C. pauciflora*, but its fragrant yellow blossoms hang in drooping clusters of 6 to 12 in spring.

Up to 5 feet high and 8 feet wide, buttercup winter hazel bears abundant pale yellow flowers.

CORYLUS AVELLANA 'CONTORTA'

KOR-i-lus a-vel-LAN-a con-TOR-ta

Harry Lauder's walking stick

6'

6'

- Strikingly gnarled and curly stems
- Interesting winter silhouette
- Showy yellow catkins
- Zones 5 to 7

Harry Lauder's walking stick becomes a dramatic living sculpture with autumn leaf drop. Native to Europe, Northern Africa, and western Asia.
USE: It's great as a focal point in entryway or courtyard, especially against a light-colored wall that silhouettes its contorted branches. Particularly effective in winter and useful in flower arrangements. Plant it with *Asarum europaeum* and chionodoxa. Growth rate: fast.
CULTURE: It adapts to a wide range of soils, acidity, and sunlight. This plant is easy to grow when you buy plants on their own roots. For grafted plants, prune vigorous suckers from below the graft union right away, or they may overtake the shrub's conspicuously twisted growth.

Eventually reaching 6 feet in height, Harry Lauder's walking stick creates an interesting focal point.

COTINUS COGGYGRIA

ko-TYE-nus ko-GIG-ree-a

Smoke tree

12'

15'

- Cloud-like flowers
- Low maintenance
- Medium texture in leaf
- Zones 5 to 8

Blossoms like puffs of pinkish, whitish or purple smoke and an open, rounded, irregular habit give smoke tree exotic appeal. Native from southern Europe to central China.
USE: It can be planted in the shrub border as a textural and color accent and in masses and groups. Species has blue-green leaves and sometimes outstanding fall color in reds, yellows, and purples. Combine with *Rudbeckia* 'Goldsturm' and *Echinacea purpurea*. Growth rate: moderate.
CULTURE: Adapts to a variety of soils, including dry, rocky ones. Needs full sun. Water it often and deeply when young; it is drought tolerant when established. Prune only to remove dead branches.
RECOMMENDED CULTIVARS: 'Velvet Cloak' retains its purple leaf color as the season progresses and has great red-purple fall color. 'Royal Purple' is the darkest purple non-fading cultivar. 'Daydream' is an especially floriferous form with pink pedicels.

Smoke tree grows 8 to 12 feet tall with clouds of pink flowers in summer. Inset right: 'Royal Purple'.

COTONEASTER SPECIES

ka-TOH-nee-as-ter

Cotoneaster

- Lustrous leaves
- Pink or white flowers followed by red berries
- Spreading habit
- Zones 5 to 8, depending on species

A handsome and versatile shrub, cotoneaster suits many garden styles and conditions. Native to China.

USE: Use it as a ground cover, in masses or in the shrub border. Growth rate: fast.

CULTURE: Cotoneaster is adaptable to many soils but prefers well-drained soil in a sunny, airy location.

RELATED SPECIES:

C. dammeri (bearberry cotoneaster) is one of the best hardy broad-leaved evergreens for ground covering because of its attractive leaves, good fruiting color, rapid growth, and low, prostrate habit. White flowers bloom in May, followed by small red berries. It spreads to 6 feet or more and remains under 1½ feet high. It is a good choice for dry, rocky soil in a sunny place. 'Lowfast' is hardy to southern zone 5. 'Coral Beauty' flowers and fruits freely. 'Streib's Finding' has a low, prostrate habit.

C. divaricatus (spreading cotoneaster) is one of the most handsome cotoneasters for summer and fall foliage, fruit, and graceful form. It grows 5 to 6 feet high and 6 to 8 feet wide. Rose-colored flowers in May are followed by red fruit from September to November. Fall colors are fluorescent in yellow and red. It prefers moist, well-drained soil, but also performs well on dry, rocky, windy sites, making it a good choice for the seashore.

C. horizontalis (rock cotoneaster) can be planted to spill over walls, down slopes, and over rocks. The angular, layered form and herringbone branches of the rock cotoneaster add an unusual texture to the garden. It can control erosion. Fall color is red except in mild climates, where the leaves remain a glossy green all winter.

C. multiflorus (many-flowered cotoneaster) is one of the most trouble-free of the cotoneasters, as well as one of the most beautiful. May flowers are followed by red berries that persist through October. This is a graceful, arching, mounded or fountain-like shrub growing 8 to 12 feet high and 12 to 15 feet wide. Use it in the shrub border or for massing. Blue-green leaves have little to no fall color.

C. salicifolius (willowleaf cotoneaster; zones 6 to 8). Another large, arching cotoneaster similar to *C. multiflorus*, but with elongated, dark green leaves. Good for large-scale massing in southern gardens. Bright red berries are attractive all winter.

Fruit display of Cotoneaster horizontalis

Cotoneaster horizontalis 'Variegatus'

Cotoneaster dammeri 'Coral Beauty'

Fruit display of Cotoneaster dammeri

Winter fruits on Cotoneaster salicifolius

Cotoneaster multiflorus

Fruit display of Cotoneaster multiflorus

Fruit display of Cotoneaster divaricatus

CYTISUS X PRAECOX

SIT-i-sus PREE-koks

Warminster Broom

4'
4'

- Year-round color
- Profuse pale yellow flowers
- Medium-fine texture
- Zones 6 to 8

This large shrub has evergreen, grass-like stems, sparse deciduous leaves, and pale yellow flowers. Hybrid origin.

USE: Plant it anywhere for evergreen accent in winter and a showy spring display. Plant it with *Aurinia saxatilis, Iberis sempervirens,* and ornamental grasses. Growth rate: fast.

CULTURE: Dry, infertile, poor soil Tip-pinch young plants, but older plants should develop their own natural form.

RECOMMENDED CULTIVARS AND RELATED SPECIES: 'Gold Spear' produces abundant yellow blooms. 'Hollandia' is a 4-foot shrub with prolific pink blossoms. *C. decumbens* (prostrate broom) is a low, creeping form with golden-yellow flowers in spring, useful for ground cover. Common broom (*C. scoparius*) is a 6-foot shrub with golden yellow flowers.

Spectacular in bloom, Warminster broom is pleasing all year with its evergreen, grass-like stems.

DAPHNE CNEORUM

DAF-nee nee-OH-rum

Rose daphne

1'
3'

- Finely textured evergreen foliage
- Perfumed flowers
- Low, trailing mass
- Zones 5 to 7

This spring-bloomer is one of the most fragrant shrubs available. Native to central and southern Europe.

USE: Rose daphne can serve as a small-scale ground cover, in a rock garden, in shady spots, near entrances, or in groupings. It looks good with *Lonicera fragrantissima* and rhododendrons. Growth rate: slow.

CULTURE: It performs best in well-drained, pH neutral soil, protected from hot sun and drying winds. Plant high to reduce chance of crown rot. Don't cultivate or move it after it is established.

RECOMMENDED CULTIVARS AND RELATED SPECIES: 'Variegata' has cream-edged foliage. *D. × burkwoodii* (zones 4 to 7) has extremely fragrant flowers that open white in May. Compact, rounded to about 3 feet high and wide. 'Carol Mackie' has green leaves edged in pale yellow, grows in sun or light shade.

Rose daphne makes a mound of 8-inch-tall trailing shoots in the rock garden. Inset: Carol Mackie daphne.

DAPHNE ODORA

DAF-nee oh-DOH-rah

Winter daphne

3'
3'

- Rosy pink flowers
- Lustrous leaves
- Compact shrub
- Zones 8 to 10

Winter daphne blooms in February and March, and has 3-inch-long leaves. Sweet, lemony scent.

USE: A sometimes difficult plant that can thrive in shady woodland conditions. Excellent in foundation plantings or in borders near walks or patios. Growth rate: slow.

CULTURE: Give winter daphne perfect drainage, water it infrequently during the summer, and plant it high. In colder regions, this evergreen should be given wall protection. Protect from winter sun and wind. May be short lived.

RELATED SPECIES: 'Alba' has white flowers. 'Aureo-marginata' has yellow-margined green leaves and is a little more cold hardy. February daphne (*D. mezereum*; zones 5 to 8) produces purple flowers before shrub is in leaf. Deciduous leaves sprout on vertically branched shrub 3 to 5 feet high; it flowers in late March or early April. Red fruits are attractive but poisonous.

Reaching 5 feet in height, Daphne odora 'Aureomarginata' combines fragrant flowers and colorful leaves.

DEUTZIA GRACILIS

DOOT-see-a gra-SIL-iss

Slender deutzia

Deutzia × rosea is slow-growing but eventually becomes a 5-foot-tall dense mound of upright branches.

- A low, broad, mounded shrub with arching branches
- Pure white flowers
- Medium texture
- Zones 5 to 8

Grow this traditional favorite for its dependably lavish white blossoms in May. Native to Japan.
USE: Plant easy-to-grow deutzia in the mixed shrub border where its plain appearance when not in bloom can blend with other shrubs. Combine it with *Muscari azureum* and *Galium odoratum*. Growth rate: slow to medium.
CULTURE: Grow deutzia in any good garden soil in full sun to light shade. Prune winter dieback immediately after flowering, since deutzia blooms on old growth. It can start growing quite early in some areas and may be damaged by late-spring frosts.
RECOMMENDED CULTIVARS AND RELATED SPECIES: 'Nikko' is a dwarf cultivar that grows 12 to 18 inches tall and 2 to 3 feet wide. *D. × rosea* 'Carminea' is a dwarf with profuse rosy pink flowers on arching branches. *D. × lemoinei* is a twiggy, erect shrub 5 to 7 feet tall with white flowers that appear after those of slender deutzia. *D. scabra* 'Codsall Pink' grows to 5 to 7 feet tall, with double pink flowers and orange-brown bark.

ELAEAGNUS PUNGENS

ell-ee-AG-nus PUN-jens

Silverberry

- Evergreen foliage
- Powerfully fragrant flowers in October
- Zones 7 to 10

Silverberry—which is a thorny evergreen with olive-colored leaves (speckled with brown beneath)—is an excellent barrier shrub for hot, dry climates and poor soil. Native to Japan.
USE: Use it as a hedge or barrier. Good in heat, wind, and drought. Provides excellent shelter in exposed and coastal situations. Plant this spreading shrub with *Arctostaphylos* species and *Callistemon citrinus*. Growth rate: very fast.
CULTURE: Prefers poor, infertile soil. Without pruning, it rapidly becomes a rigid, sprawling, angular shrub 6 to 16 feet tall. Should be pruned as necessary to restrict its vigorous growth.
RECOMMENDED CULTIVARS: 'Aurea' has yellow edges on the leaves. 'Fruitlandii' has rounder, larger, wavy-edged leaves with silver below, and a more symmetrical outline than the species. Handsome 'Maculata' creates a very bright effect with a large golden blotch in the center of each leaf. 'Variegata' is similar to 'Aurea' but with paler yellow narrowly edging the margins.

Silverberry can reach 16 feet in height, with fragrant flowers in autumn. Shown here: 'Maculata'.

ENKIANTHUS CAMPANULATUS

en-kee-AN-thus cam-pan-u-LAY-tus

Redvein enkianthus

- Flowers in May
- Red fall color
- Interesting horizontal branching structure
- Zones 5 to 8

A refined upright shrub, redvein enkianthus produces delicate, yellowish clusters of bell-like flowers that become veined with red. Leaves turn various shades of orange-red in autumn. Native to Japan.
USE: It can be used as a specimen, and combines well with rhododendrons and *Pieris japonica*. Put it near entryways and outdoor living areas. Perfectly suited to an open position in the woodland garden. Flowers last a long time in arrangements. Growth rate: slow. It grows 6 to 8 feet tall in the North.
CULTURE: Redvein enkianthus needs moist, well-drained acid soil rich in organic matter. Plant it in full sun to partial shade. Water well during times of drought and keep it away from roadsides and beaches, where salty spray can affect its health.
RECOMMENDED CULTIVARS AND RELATED SPECIES: 'Albiflorus' has whiter flowers. *E. perulatus* is a compact shrub 6 to 7 feet high with attractive dark green leaves, intense scarlet foliage in autumn, and masses of urn-shaped, small white flowers in spring. Cold hardy only to zone 6.

Redvein enkianthus can reach 8 to 10 feet in height. Its leaves turn orange-yellow to red in the fall.

ERICA SPECIES

AIR-i-ka

Heath

1' 3'

- Fine texture
- 18 inches to 7 feet
- Colorful spring flowers
- Zones 5 to 10, zone 4 with snow cover

Native to central and southern Europe.
USE: These narrow-leaved evergreens make outstanding ground covers, masses, facing plants for the shrub border, and rock garden specimens. Plant with *Calluna vulgaris* and *Ilex crenata* 'Helleri'. Growth rate: moderate.
CULTURE: Plant it in acid, infertile, sandy or highly organic soil in full sun to partial shade.
RELATED SPECIES: *E. carnea* (spring heath; zones 6 to 8, zone 5 with reliable snow cover) is a dwarf spreader up to 16 inches high and 6 feet wide. Annual pruning after flowering will make it look its best. *E. cinerea* (Scotch heather; zones 6 to 8, zone 5 with reliable snow cover) has cultivars that flower in summer. *E. tetralix* (cross-leaved heath; Zones 5 to 8, Zone 4 with reliable snow cover) blooms mid- to late summer on 15-inch plants. *E. mediterranea* (Mediterranean heath; zones 8 to 10) has upright growth 4 to 7 feet high for an excellent fine-textured background.

Above: **Erica 'King George' blooms in spring, early enough to occasionally get caught by late snowfall (inset).**

ESCALLONIA RUBRA

ess-ka-LONE-ee-a ROO-bra

Escallonia

10'

8'

- Red flowers in summer and fall
- Evergreen foliage
- Medium texture
- Zones 8 to 10

This South American native is a tough, virtually foolproof shrub for warm coastal gardens.
USE: Screen or windbreak, or for massing and integrating into the shrub border. Plant it with *Berberis darwinii* and *Passiflora caerulea*. Growth rate: fast.
CULTURE: Plant it away from highly alkaline soils. Provide partial shade in hot inland gardens. It tolerates short periods of drought but performs best with adequate watering. Prune lightly to keep its form compact. Otherwise, it grows 6 to 13 feet tall with a dense, mounded, upright habit.
RELATED SPECIES: *Escallonia × exoniensis* 'Balfourii' (Zones 9 to 10) grows up to 10 feet tall with drooping branchlets and pink blossoms. *Escallonia × exoniensis* 'Frades' (Zones 9 to 10) produces abundant pink flowers and retains a compact habit 5 to 6 feet high.

Escallonia × exoniensis 'Frades' is a compact variety that stays a neat 5 to 6 feet tall and wide.

EUONYMUS ALATUS

yew-ON-i-mus a-LAY-tus

Burning bush

12'

15'

- Great fall color
- Vase-shaped habit
- Big corky ridges or wings on stems
- Zones 4 to 7

Beloved by gardeners for its brilliant scarlet fall color. Native from northeastern Asia to central China.
USE: Makes good unclipped hedge or screen, in groups, in the shrub border, or as a specimen. Burning bush looks good with *Sedum* 'Autumn Joy' and *Festuca ovina* 'Glauca'. Growth rate: slow.
CULTURE: Adaptable to many soils and growing conditions, except to wet ones. Full sun to heavy shade. Needs moister soil in full sun. Grows 12 to 15 feet high and wide, so leave plenty of room for it to expand. Pruning destroys its neat outline and causes uneven growth. All parts of the plant may cause stomach upset if consumed.
RECOMMENDED CULTIVARS: Dwarf burning bush 'Compacta' (zones 5 to 7) is more compact and dense and grows 10 feet high with bright pinkish-red fall color. 'Rudy Haag' grows 4 to 5 feet high with rosy red fall color.

Burning bush is one of the most reliable and recognizable deciduous shrubs for brilliant autumn color.

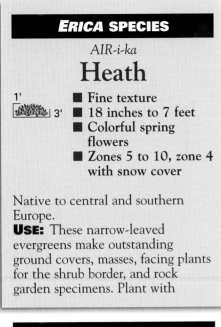

EUONYMUS FORTUNEI

yew-ON-i-mus for-TOO-nee-eye

Winter creeper euonymus

Winter creeper euonymus is one of the hardiest broadleaf evergreens. Shown here: 'Emerald 'n' Gold'.

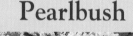 3' / 5'

- One of the hardiest broad-leaved evergreens
- Available in spreading and bushy forms
- Disease prone
- Zones 5 to 8

Wintercreeper euonymous is valued for its landscape versatility. Native to China.
USE: Plant it as a ground cover, vine, wall cover, or low hedge. Plant it with *Daphne × burkwoodii* 'Carol Mackie' and *Dicentra eximia*. Growth rate: fast.
CULTURE: Tolerant of all but the wettest soil, withstands full sun to heavy shade. Susceptible to several serious pests and diseases, especially euonymous scale. Avoid harsh, windy locations where the foliage is prone to browning in winter.
RELATED SPECIES: *E. japonicus* (Japanese euonymus) is hardy in zones 8 to 10. It becomes a small tree 15 feet high and 8 feet wide and can make a tough, low-maintenance shrub.

E. kiautschovicus (spreading euonymus) is an 8- to 10-foot high shrub in zones 8 to 9, lower in zones 6 to 7. 'Dupont' is hardier and more compact, with large leaves and robust habit, but it is susceptible to disease. 'Manhattan' is similar to 'Dupont' but with dark green shiny leaves.

EXOCHORDA RACEMOSA

eks-oh-KOR-da ra-se-MOH-sa

Pearlbush

Growing 3 to 4 feet high and wide, Exochorda macrantha 'The Bride' is a top-performing pearlbush.

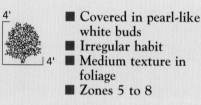 4' / 4'

- Covered in pearl-like white buds
- Irregular habit
- Medium texture in foliage
- Zones 5 to 8

A large, spreading shrub that is lovely in spring, when its many stems are cloaked with white flowers and blue-green leaves. Native to eastern China.
USE: Useful as an isolated specimen or for the spring-flowering mixed border and for the shrub border, where its rather unruly habit will be hidden after flowering. It goes well with *Calycanthus floridus* and *Deutzia × rosea* 'Carminea'.

Growth rate: moderate.
CULTURE: Plant in well-drained acid soil in full sun to partial shade with average watering. Prune annually after flowering to remove weak or crossing stems and to maintain a more compact habit and reduce crowding.
RELATED SPECIES: *E. × macrantha* 'The Bride' is an elegant, hybrid cultivar that grows 3 to 4 feet high and wider with a somewhat weeping habit and profuse white flowers in mid- to late-spring. It is slightly less cold hardy than *E. racemosa*. *E. giraldii* var. *wilsonii* (Wilson's pearlbush) is more showy, free-flowering, and slightly less cold hardy (to zone 5).

FORSYTHIA X INTERMEDIA

for-SITH-ee-a in-ter-MEE-dee-a

Border forsythia

Golden-yellow flowers cover the arching branches of Forsythia × intermedia 'Lynwood' in early spring.

 9' / 12'

- Spectacular pale to deep yellow flowers
- Upright, arching, vigorous habit
- Medium texture
- Zones 5 to 9

Easy-to-grow forsythia is a popular and very colorful shrub for forcing branches; it blooms in February, March, or April, depending on the climate. Hybrid origin.
USE: When allowed room to grow and to maintain its natural massive mounded habit, forsythia is dramatic in the distant landscape. It also can be planted with *Chaenomeles speciosa* and *Magnolia* species. Growth rate: fast.

CULTURE: It grows in any soil but requires water and feeding. Plant it in protected areas to shield flower buds from spring frosts. Prune annually after flowering by removing one-third of the oldest canes. Do not shear. Renew old plants by cutting them to the ground.
RECOMMENDED CULTIVARS AND RELATED SPECIES: 'Lynwood' and 'Spring Glory' are the most popular cultivars. *F. ovata* hybrids 'Meadow Lark' and 'Northern Gold' are cold hardy to zone 4 and floriferous with erect form. *F. suspensa* (zones 5 to 8) has a gracefully pendulous form that cascades over banks.

FOTHERGILLA MAJOR

faw-ther-GIL-la MAY-jer

Large fothergilla

8'
6'

- Honey-scented profuse blooms
- Long-lasting fall color
- Neat rounded habit
- Zones 5 to 8

A superior, low-maintenance shrub, it blooms white in April or May and has fluorescent orange, yellow, and red fall foliage. Native to the southern Appalachians.
USE: Use large fothergilla in groups, shrub borders, or as

specimens in the woodland garden. Plant it with *Betula nigra* 'Heritage' and *Sedum* 'Vera Jameson'. Growth rate: medium at first, then slow.
CULTURE: It does best in acid, well-drained soil. Grows well in partial shade, but full sun encourages more flowers and improves autumn color. Pest- and disease-free, it requires no special care.
RELATED SPECIES: Dwarf fothergilla (*F. gardenii*; zones 5 to 8) is similar except for size (3 to 5 feet tall) and flowers, which are smaller and appear before the leaves. It is a very pretty, fine plant for smaller spaces. 'Blue Mist' has blue-green leaves. 'Mount Airy' grows to 5 feet tall with outstanding fall color and

profuse flowers. 'Jane Platt' is a dwarf, 3 feet high.

Large fothergilla reaches 8 feet in height and bears white flower spikes. Inset: dwarf fothergilla in fall.

FUCHSIA HYBRIDS

FEW-shya HIBE-rid-a

Common fuchsia

3'
3'

- Flamboyant multicolored flowers
- Shrubby to cascading
- Medium texture
- Zones 10 to 11

This fuchsia flowers from early summer to frost and attracts hummingbirds when grown outdoors in zone 10. Hybrid origin.
USE: Espalier, upright specimen for the rock garden, or shrub border. Plant it with *Escallonia rubra* and

Berberis darwinii. Growth rate: fast.
CULTURE: Best in areas with cool summers, high atmospheric moisture, filtered shade, and moist, rich soil. Mulch heavily, mist, and water frequently in dry climates. Protect from hot, searing winds. Apply liquid fertilizer lightly every 10 to 14 days throughout the growing season. Pinch stems back frequently to encourage dense growth. Prune annually in early spring before new growth starts, keeping at least two healthy buds on each branch.
RELATED SPECIES: Hardy fuchsia (*F. magellanica*; zones 6 to 10) grows to a graceful, rounded, 3-foot shrub each year in the North after dying

back in winter (4 to 8 feet tall in the Deep South). It bears profuse, bright red flowers with blue inner petals, smaller than those of common fuchsia.

Hardy fuchsia (inset) is a delicate, smaller-flowered version of the more tender hybrids (above).

GARDENIA JASMINOIDES

gar-DEE-nee-a jas-min-OY-deez

Gardenia

6'
6'

- Magnificent fragrance
- Large, waxy, white flowers
- Glossy evergreen
- Zones 8 to 10

An intensely fragrant, beautiful shrub worth the maintenance it requires. Native to China.
USE: Use as specimens in containers, raised beds, hedges, low screens, or espaliers. Gardenia is gorgeous with Bourbon and tea roses. Growth rate: moderate.

CULTURE: Avoid alkaline soil, poor drainage, and drought. Plant crowns high in acid soil rich in organic matter in a site protected from full sun. Mist regularly in early morning while plant is not in bloom. Feed every 3 to 4 weeks with an acid plant food. Spray regularly to control sucking insects. Best in areas with warm evenings, Gardenias do not bloom well in cool-summer climates.
RECOMMENDED CULTIVARS: 'Radicans' has a prostrate habit that makes it an effective ground cover on a limited scale. 'Radicans Variegata' is similar to 'Radicans' but with creamy white to pale yellow leaf margins. 'August Beauty'

is a robust shrub 4 to 6 feet tall with big, profuse, double white flowers.

Pure white, waxy blossoms of the gardenia can perfume the entire garden. It grows 6 to 8 feet tall.

HAMAMELIS X INTERMEDIA

ham-a-MEAL-is in-ter-MEE-dee-a

Hybrid witch hazel

15'

15'

- Red, orange, and yellow foliage in fall
- Yellow, red flowers
- Spicily fragrant
- Zones 5 to 8

Above: Hamamelis 'Diane' in fall. Right, top: 'Ruby Glow'; right, bottom: Japanese witch hazel.

Spider-shaped flowers are produced in winter to early spring on leafless branches and can withstand long periods of extreme cold without damage or injury, Very attractive autumn color. Hybrid origin.

USE: Excellent for the naturalized woodland, or as a specimen plant located near windows to provide a glimpse of spring. Also effective when planted in groups in the shrub border or in the woodland garden. Combine witch hazel with *Cornus mas* and *Lamium galeobdolon*. Growth rate: slow.

CULTURE: Plant in deep rich soil with an abundant supply of moisture in full sun to partial shade. This pest-free plant needs occasional deep watering during droughts. Pruning is simply a matter of removing any dead wood.

RECOMMENDED CULTIVARS AND RELATED SPECIES: 'Arnold Promise': bright medium-sized yellow flowers. 'Jelena': yellow flowers suffused with copper, and orange, red, and scarlet fall color. 'Diane': deep red flowers and superb rich-red fall color. Common witch hazel (*H. virginiana*; zones 5 to 9): 15 to 20 feet high and wide, with yellow flowers in October and November and clear yellow fall foliage. Japanese witch hazel (*H. japonica*; zones 5 to 8): fragrant yellow flowers and yellow fall color.

HEBE

HEE-bee

Shrubby veronica

3'

5'

- Bottlebrush flower
- Long bloom period
- Green, silver, or creamy-variegated evergreen foliage
- Zones 8 to 10
- Invaluable for seashore areas

Above: 'Patty's Purple'; inset: 'C.B. Anderson'. Hebe is popular for its long season of color in mild climates.

Shrubby veronica produces mauve, red, purple, blue, or white flowers from early summer to late fall, and serves well in small gardens on the south and west coasts. Native to New Zealand.

USE: Cultivated for its flowers and evergreen foliage, shrubby veronica is useful for bedding, containers, and difficult sites—including rock gardens—where few other plants will thrive. Shrubby veronica is useful as both a hedging and as a ground cover in coastal areas. Combine it with *Lonicera nitida* and *Callistemon citrinus*. Growth rate: fast.

CULTURE: It is adaptable to any well-drained soil in full sun, including seashore conditions. Keep this shrub neat with occasional trimming. Prune to renew every four to five years.

RELATED SPECIES: *Hebe* 'Autumn Glory' has compact growth to 2 feet high and wide with 2-inch, deep lavender-blue flower spikes in late summer and fall. Its small round leaves are deep green and tinged with purple. *H. buxifolia* is a rounded form to 5 feet tall and wide. It has white flowers in small clusters in summer and is one of the hardier hebes; it can be planted to zone 8. The selection 'Patty's Purple' has deep purple flowers on red stalks. *H. cupressoides* boasts long, slender, green or gray branches remarkably like those of a cypress. Its pale blue flowers are small. The selection 'Boughton Dome' is a compact form with white flowers. *H. pimeleoides* 'Quicksilver' is a dwarf, spreading shrub with small, silvery-blue leaves that contrast quite nicely with the dark shoots and pale purple blossoms. *H. salicifolia* is a 10-foot-tall seaside shrub with fragrant lilac-purple bottlebrushes and willowy lance-shaped leaves. *H. speciosa* is a small, dense rounded shrub with purple flower spikes and leathery leaves. 'Midsummer Beauty', a speciosa hybrid, has fragrant lavender flower spikes and red-tinted leaf bottoms. The selection 'Variegata' has leaves splashed with cream and gray-green.

HEPTACODIUM MICONIOIDES

hep-ta-KOH-dee-um mi-ko-nee-OY-deez

Seven-son flower

12'
8'

- Tan, exfoliating bark
- Fragrant, delicate white flowers
- Rose to purple sepals
- Zones 6 to 8

An increasingly popular shrub from western China, seven-son flower has an upright, multi-stemmed habit and provides year-round interest. White flowers in late summer are followed by showy rose-purple sepals that remain effective for a month or more. Prized for its attractive, peeling light tan to brown bark; dark green leaves become purple-tinged in fall.

USE: Nice in shrub borders, where its legginess can be faced down with shorter shrubs. Works well in urban gardens with good tolerance for drought and salt conditions. Plant with blue hydrangeas and azaleas. Growth rate: fast.

CULTURE: Flowers best in well-drained, acid soil in full sun but also grows in partial or dappled shade and alkaline soil. Withstands some drought. Water sparingly in winter. Cut out dead or broken branches when necessary.

Seven-son flower produces white, fragrant flowers in late summer, followed by dramatic rosy sepals.

HIBISCUS SYRIACUS

high-BISS-kus see-ree-AY-kus

Rose of Sharon

12'
10'

- Flowers in white, red, purple, and violet
- Medium texture
- Shrub or small tree
- Zones 5 to 9

Grow this popular round-topped, erect shrub for late-season flowers 2 to 4 inches wide. Native to China and India.

USE: Use grouped or massed in a shrub border. Plant it in with *Juniperus conferta* and *Rosa rugosa*. Growth rate: moderate.

CULTURE: Salt and wind tolerant. Thrives in well-drained soil and in full sun and tolerates partial shade. Susceptible to insects in humid climates. Prune to two or three buds per stem each spring for increased flowers.

RECOMMENDED CULTIVARS AND RELATED SPECIES: 'Diana' has clear white ruffled flowers, 'Bluebird' has light violet-blue flowers. 'Minerva' has dark red eye spot and lavender petals tinged pink. Chinese hibiscus (*H. rosa-sinensis*; zones 9 to 10) has crimson flowers and grows fast to 30 feet high with moist, well-drained soil, sun, heat, and protection from wind and frost.

Often the size of small trees, rose of Sharon blooms midsummer to fall. Left: 'Diana'; right: 'Bluebird'.

HIPPOPHAE RHAMNOIDES

HIP-o-figh ram-NOY-deez

Sea buckthorn

20'
15'

- Orange fruit clusters
- Spreading, suckering, thorny habit
- Lance-like leaves
- Zones 3 to 7

Sea buckthorn makes a valuable addition to the seaside garden, with female plants producing tiny yellow-green flowers followed by edible bright orange fruit (both male and female plants are needed to produce fruit). Linear leaves are dark gray-green on top and lustrous silver on bottom. Native to Europe and Asia.

USE: Good, low-maintenance plant for borders and massing. Works well in a shrub or mixed border, as a specimen plant, as well as in the wild garden. Plant sea buckthorn in combination with *Tamarix* species and *Cotoneaster divaricatus*. Growth rate: fast.

CULTURE: It grows best in full sun. Tolerates salty and wet conditions. Succeeds in almost any soil. For fruit, plant one male buckthorn for every half-dozen females. Prune in late summer, however pruning is seldom necessary. Because it is difficult to transplant, use care and consideration when siting.

Reaching 20 feet high and wide, sea buckthorn can be used as a hedge as well as to stabilize sand dunes.

HYDRANGEA ARBORESCENS

hy-DRAN-jya ar-bor-ESS-enz

Smooth hydrangea

Smooth hydrangea is one of the most popular hydrangeas. Shown here: the giant-flowered 'Annabelle'.

- Rounded, creamy flower cluster 4 to 6 inches wide
- Bold textured
- Low, clumpy habit
- Zones 3 to 9

Long-lasting, lavish flowers from midsummer to early fall, which can be used in dried arrangements, grow on a tough, multistemmed shrub. Native from New York to Florida.

USE: Smooth hydrangeas are good for a range of garden sites. They work well in group plantings or as a single specimen, in a shrub border, or even in containers. Plant in combination with *Ilex glabra* and *Prunus maritima*. Growth rate: fast.

CULTURE: Prefers well-drained, moist soil rich in organic matter. It does best in partial shade but adapts well to full sun if kept watered. Salt tolerant and pH adaptable. It flowers on new growth, so prune in late fall or early spring to keep it compact. Provide shelter from cold, drying winds. Contact with the foliage may irritate skin.

RECOMMENDED CULTIVARS:
'Grandiflora' bears creamy-white 4- to 6-inch snowball clusters from midsummer to early autumn. 'Annabelle' is the most commonly grown variety. It is a showy, compact, 4-foot shrub with huge, spectacular, rounded heads of white, as much as 12 inches or more across. Blooms best in full sun. Leaves are medium green and large.

HYDRANGEA MACROPHYLLA

hy-DRAN-jya mak-row-FILL-a

Bigleaf hydrangea

- Rounded, suckering shrub
- White, pink, or blue flowers
- Coarse in leaf
- Zone 7 to 10 (zone 6 along the East Coast)

Bigleaf hydrangea is valued for its late-summer floral display and lustrous neat leaves in mild-winter areas. Native to Japan.

USE: Good for foundations and facing down taller, leggy shrubs, as well as in the shrub border. Excellent seaside plant, especially in the South. Combine it with *Lagerstroemia indica* and *Clethra alnifolia*. Growth rate: fast.

CULTURE: Plant in full sun at the shore or in partial shade and moist, rich, well-drained soil high in organic matter. The soil's acidity affects the plant's uptake of aluminum, which in turn determines whether the flowers are pink or blue. For bluer flowers, provide extra acidity and aluminum (aluminum sulfate is good). For pink flowers apply lime to decrease soil acidity. Prune after flowering only to remove flower heads. It flowers on the previous year's growth.

RECOMMENDED CULTIVARS:
Many cultivars are available, differing by hardiness (some are reportedly hardy to zone 5, while others have been bred as pot plants for greenhouses), length of bloom (some begin blooming earlier for a longer season), size (dwarf 2-foot mounds to large 5-foot shrubs), foliage color (some are variegated), flower color (blue, white, pink, and red), and flower form (the "hortensia" group bears globe-shaped flower clusters composed of many large, sterile florets; the "lace-cap" group bears tight clusters of tiny florets circled by a ring of large, sterile florets). Some of the most garden-worthy varieties are: 'All Summer Beauty', a compact (to 3 feet) early-bloomer with dark blue flowers; 'Blue Billow', with violet-and-white lace-cap blooms; 'Forever Pink', a compact 3-foot hortensia with flowers that remain pink even in acid soils; 'Glowing Embers', a bright red hortensia; 'Mariesii Variegata', a blue lacecap with ivory-variegated leaves; and 'Nikko Blue', a large bright-blue hortensia.

Above: 'Gentian Dome'. Center: 'Laranth White' in fall and 'Blue Wave' (inset). Right: 'All Summer Beauty' and 'Forever Pink (inset).

HYDRANGEA PANICULATA

hy-DRAN-jya pa-nik-u-LAY-ta

Panicle hydrangea

22'
20'

- Conical flower panicles 6 to 8 inches long
- Coarse texture
- Spreading shrub
- Zones 3 to 8

This large shrub or small tree is an old-fashioned favorite for its long season of bloom, with branches that arch from the weight of its cone-shaped flower clusters. The white flowers appear in midsummer, changing through shades of pink, buff, and rust from late summer into fall. Native to Japan.

USE: Plant it in the shrub border, where its coarseness will not be as prominent, or prune it to form a small tree. Combine it with *Ceratostigma plumbaginoides*, *Sedum* 'Autumn Joy' and *Ilex crenata* 'Helleri'. Growth rate: fast.

CULTURE: Moist, well-drained soil with plenty of organic matter in sun or partial shade. It flowers on new growth, so prune in winter or early spring, removing weak or dead stems. Vigorous and trouble-free.

RECOMMENDED CULTIVARS: 'Grandiflora' (sometimes called "pee gee hydrangea") has "snowball" type clusters, elongated to 8 to 10 inches, which turn pink in late summer and brown in autumn. 'Unique' bears especially large, 12-inch-long flower clusters over an even longer period than the species.

Panicle hydrangea can reach a height of 22 feet. Above: 'Pink Diamond' in fall. Right: 'Grandiflora'.

HYDRANGEA QUERCIFOLIA

hy-DRAN-jya kwer-si-FOH-li-a

Oakleaf hydrangea

6'
8'

- Bold leaves
- Flowers to 1 foot long
- Shaggy bark is decorative in winter
- Zones 5 to 8

Burgundy and purple leaves provide fall color, and dry flowers stay on the plant into winter. Flowers are greenish pink to brown. Native to the southeastern United States.

USE: A fine addition to the shrub border, oakleaf hydrangea also provides a strong accent in large masses. It performs well in sun or shade and in mass or as a specimen. Plant it with *Fothergilla major* and *Dicentra eximia*. Growth rate: slow to moderate.

CULTURE: Plant in moist, fertile, well-drained, acid soil in sun or half shade. Also tolerates dense shade but produces fewer flowers and less intense fall color. In zones 7 to 8 it requires shade. Mulch well in dry climates to keep the roots cool and moist.

RECOMMENDED CULTIVARS: 'Snow Queen' has larger flower heads (with larger individual florets) that are held more upright for greater show. Plant is more compact (5 to 7 feet tall and wide), and fall color is good. 'Snowflake' has double florets, with a set of smaller sepals within the larger ones, making a unique display. 'Pee Wee' is 30 to 40 inches and produces excellent flowers.

Oakleaf hydrangea can reach 6 feet high and 8 feet wide. Left: 'Snow Queen'. Above: fall foliage.

HYPERICUM PROLIFICUM

hy-PEAR-i-kum pro-LIH-fi-kum

Shrubby
St. Johnswort

St. Johnswort is one of the easiest shrubs to grow. Above: 'Sunburst'. Inset: H. × moseranum 'Tricolor'.

3'
4'

- Bluish green leaves
- Dense, rounded shrub
- Bright yellow flowers
- Medium-fine texture
- Zones 4 to 9

Compact, low-maintenance shrub flowers from mid-June through August. Native from New Jersey to Iowa and Georgia.

USE: This plants works well in foundation plantings, shrub borders in front of taller shrubs, mixed borders, or in masses. Plant it with *Potentilla fruticosa* and *Pennisetum alopecuroides*. Growth rate: slow.

CULTURE: Shrubby St. Johnswort does best in full sun and light, well-drained soil, but tolerates poor, dry, sterile soil, air pollution, and partial shade. Prune infrequently in late spring after new growth hardens off.

RELATED SPECIES: *H. × frondosum* 'Sunburst' (golden St. Johnswort; zones 5 to 9) has handsome blue-green foliage. It is a 3- to 4-foot-high shrub with large bright yellow flowers. *H. × patulum* (goldencup St. Johnswort; zones 7 to 10) is a semievergreen or evergreen shrub 3 feet high and wide. 'Hidcote' is an 18-inch shrub in zones 5 to 6, with large yellow flowers from late June to September. In zones 7 to 9, it is less likely to kill back and reaches 3 to 4 feet, flowering both on old and new growth, from May to October.

Evergreen candytuft is a handsome year-round ground cover for sunny spots and well-drained soil.

IBERIS SEMPERVIRENS

IH-ber-is sem-per-VY-renz

Evergreen
candytuft

1'
2'

- Showy, pure white flowers in spring
- Dwarf evergreen
- Low, spreading habit
- Zones 5 to 10

Handsome plant forms a mat of dark green, fine-textured foliage. Native to southern Europe and western Asia.

USE: Candytuft can be planted as a ground cover with woody shrubs and spring bulbs. Combine with *Abelia × grandiflora* 'Prostrata' and *Ajuga reptans* 'Burgundy Glow'. Excellent with rhododendrons. Growth rate: slow to moderate.

CULTURE: It prefers light, well-drained soil with average fertility, in sun to light shade. Prune it hard each year after flowering and do not overfertilize. Removing spent flowers increases the next year's bloom and keeps plants dense.

RECOMMENDED CULTIVARS: 'Autumn Snow' blooms again in autumn. 'Little Gem' is shorter and hardier than the species. 'Purity' and 'Snowflake' have larger flower clusters. 'Snowmantle' is an especially vigorous variety.

ILEX CORNUTA

EYE-leks kor-NOO-ta

Chinese holly

Two of the many varieties of Chinese holly: the red-berried 'Dazzler' (left) and the yellow-berried 'D'Or' (right).

12'
12'

- Upright rounded shrub
- Evergreen leaves
- Profuse red berries
- Zones 7 to 9

Popular compact cultivars have bold, handsome, glossy foliage. Native to Eastern China and Korea.

USE: Cultivars used for foundations, hedges, and shrub borders. Plant it with *Nandina domestica* and *Prunus laurocerasus*. Growth rate: slow to moderate.

CULTURE: Prefers moist, well-drained, slightly acid soils in sun or shade. Drought, heat, pH, and pollution tolerant. Male and female plants are needed for berries.

RECOMMENDED CULTIVARS AND RELATED SPECIES: 'Burfordii' is a dense, round shrub that grows 10 to 15 feet high and fruits heavily without pollination. 'Dwarf Burford' is a compact 6-foot form. 'Carissa' is a male dwarf that grows 2 to 3 feet high. 'Dazzler' is a compact female, under 10 feet, with superb fruit display. *I. × merserveae* is an 8-foot evergreen hardy to zone 6 (some cultivars to zone 5), with glossy dark blue-green foliage. 'Blue Princess' has dark red berries; 'Blue Prince' is a male pollinator. 'China Girl' is a hybrid of *I. cornuta* and *I. rugosa*, with brighter green foliage and red berries. 'China Boy' is the male pollinator.

ILEX CRENATA

EYE-leks kren-AH-ta

Japanese holly

10' | 12'

- Lustrous, dark evergreen foliage
- Neat rounded shape
- Fine texture
- Zones 6 south to 10, some cultivars to zone 5

Native to Japan.
USE: Excellent for hedges, foundation plantings, massing, and shrub borders. Use it with *Rhododendron kaempferi* and *Thuja occidentalis* 'Globosa'. Fruit is black, inconspicuous. Growth rate: slow.
CULTURE: It does best in moist but well-drained, slightly acidic soil in sun or shade. Pollution tolerant. It can be sheared into formal shapes. Prune after new growth matures in spring.
RECOMMENDED CULTIVARS: 'Beehive' is a rounded dwarf with bright green foliage. 'Convexa' has small convex leaves that sparkle, and is hardy to zone 6. 'Dwarf Pagoda' is a picturesque dwarf with closely packed leaves, suitable for bonsai. 'Glory' has small, flat leaves, and is unusually cold hardy, to zone 5. 'Helleri' has small leaves and is very dwarf, 2 to 3 feet high. 'Hetzii' is similar to 'Convexa' but with larger leaves, hardy to zone 6. 'Microphylla' has small leaves. 'Midas Touch' has yellow leaf margins.

Japanese holly is a small-leaved evergreen useful for hedges and topiary. Shown here: 'Hetzii'.

ILEX GLABRA

EYE-leks GLAY-bra

Inkberry

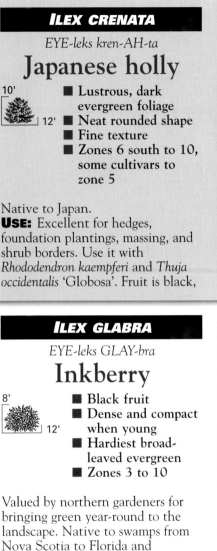
8' | 12'

- Black fruit
- Dense and compact when young
- Hardiest broad-leaved evergreen
- Zones 3 to 10

Valued by northern gardeners for bringing green year-round to the landscape. Native to swamps from Nova Scotia to Florida and Mississippi.
USE: A fine shrub for massing, hedges, and foundation planting. Salt-tolerant; excellent for the seashore. Plant it with *Myrica pensylvanica* and *Rosa rugosa*. Growth rate: slow to medium.
CULTURE: It grows well in moist but well-drained soil, in full sun to part shade. Responds well to shearing; prune heavily to renew leggy old plants. Generally pest-resistant and trouble-free.
RECOMMENDED CULTIVARS: 'Compacta', Densa', 'Nordic' and 'Shamrock' are all compact forms.

Inkberry is the most cold-hardy of all broadleaf evergreens. 'Densa', shown above, is a compact form.

ILEX VERTICILLATA

EYE-leks ver-tih-sih-LAY-ta

Common winterberry

8' | 10'

- Deciduous holly
- Outstanding bright red berries
- Happy in wet soil
- Zones 4 to 8

Fruit of winterberry persists into the winter on bare branches, attracting birds in the eastern United States. Native to North American swamps in the East and Midwest.
USE: Effective in masses in the shrub border and by water. Combine winterberry with *Viburnum dilatatum* and *Aronia arbutifolia*. Growth rate: slow.
CULTURE: It does best in moist to wet soil, high in organic matter, and in full sun to partial shade. Plant a male within 10 to 15 feet of female plants to ensure pollination.
RECOMMENDED CULTIVARS: 'Afterglow' grows 4 to 6 feet tall, with large orange-red fruits. 'Aurantiaca' grows 3 to 5 feet tall with red, then yellow-orange fruits. 'Jim Dandy' is a low-growing male that will pollinate 'Afterglow', 'Aurantiaca', and 'Red Sprite'. 'Red Sprite' (also called 'Nana') grows to only 2 to 4 feet tall, with very large red fruits. 'Southern Gentleman' is a male growing 4 to 6 feet tall that will pollinate 'Winter Red'. 'Winter Red' grows 8 to 10 feet high and wide, with abundant red fruit.

The 2-foot 'Red Sprite' winterberry is the smallest variety with the largest red berries. Birds love this plant.

JUNIPERUS

joo-NIH-pur-us

Junipers

- Fine texture
- Low maintenance
- Shrubby, prostrate, or columnar cultivars
- Zones vary with the species

Worldwide, there are about 70 species of junipers, 17 of which are native to the United States. They have two types of leaves: sharp needle-like juvenile leaves, or blunt, scalelike mature leaves, varying with the species. Junipers are adaptable to almost any conditions, notably to hot, dry sites, but sometimes are infested with mites and bagworms. Some are susceptible to juniper blight (*Phomopsis*).

USE: Cultivars make good ground covers, accents, and border plants. Plant shrubby and spreading junipers with *Miscanthus* species, ophiopogons, yuccas, and cytisus. Growth rate: slow to medium, variable by cultivar.

CULTURE: Best in well-drained soil and full sun, but adaptable to average moisture and partial shade. Place them away from lawn sprinklers and in general avoid overwatering.

J. chinensis (Chinese juniper; zones 4 to 10) tolerates alkaline soil. It is slightly susceptible to juniper blight, moderately so in very wet years. Native to China, Mongolia, and Japan. 'San Jose' is a low form 2 feet high and 8 to 10 feet wide.

J. communis (common juniper; zones 3 to 7, depending on geographical origin) typically grows 5 to 10 feet high and 8 to 12 feet wide. It has only spiny juvenile foliage, dull to blue-green in summer and brownish to purplish in winter. Common juniper is native to more places than any other shrub or tree, including northern and central Europe, the Mediterranean region, Asia Minor, Iran, Afghanistan, the western Himalayas, Canada, the eastern United States from New England to North Carolina and west to the Rockies, and California. Subspecies *alpina* includes low-growing alpine plants with good blue-green color year-round or purplish color in winter. Cultivars include 'Berkshire' (Massachusetts) and 'Gold Beach' (California), a fine ground cover. Subspecies *depressa* includes vase-shaped plants, a few of which are useful. 'Compressa' is a slow-growing form 2 to 3 feet high and wide, and 'Depressa Aurea' is more vigorous, with golden branch tips.

J. conferta (shore juniper; zones 6 to 10) is an excellent ground cover, especially for coastal sites. It has bluish green, soft-looking but prickly foliage and a dense, mat-like growth habit, 1 to 2 feet tall and 6 to 8 feet wide. Shore Juniper is native to the seacoast of Japan.

J. horizontalis (creeping juniper;

Juniperus chinensis *'San Jose'*

Juniperus communis *'Depressa Aurea'*

Juniperus conferta *'Blue Pacific'*

Juniperus horizontalis *'Bar Harbor'*

Juniperus × media *'Hetzii'*

Juniperus procumbens *'Nana'*

Zones 3 to 9) is a low-spreading ground cover with silvery blue-green foliage that turns purple in winter. Some cultivars are highly susceptible to juniper blight. It is native from Nova Scotia to British Columbia and south to Montana and Massachusetts. 'Bar Harbor', 'Wiltonii' ('Blue Rug'), 'Douglasii', and 'Blue Chip' are blue-green in summer, silvery blue or purple in winter, and grow 6 to 8 inches high.

 J. × media (hybrid juniper; zones 4 to 9) 10' includes cultivars that once were assigned to J. chinensis, but now are believed to be hybrids with J. sabina. 'Armstrong' is upright to 5 to 6 feet, with olive-green foliage. 'Hetzii' grows 8 to 10 feet and more high and 20 feet or more wide, with silvery blue-green foliage. 'Mint Julep' grows 2 to 3 feet high, spreading 6 feet wide, with bright green foliage. 'Pfitzeriana' grows 6 to 8 feet high and 15 feet wide, with grayish olive-green foliage.

 J. procumbens 15' (Japanese garden juniper; zones 5 to 9) is a ground cover that grows 1 to 2 feet high and spreads indefinitely very wide. It has soft blue-green needle-like juvenile foliage. While it is a popular ground cover, this plant is very susceptible to juniper blight. 'Nana' grows to 1 foot.

 J. sabina (savin 6' juniper; zones 5 to 9) has bright to deep green foliage that turns brown in winter. Pollution tolerant and blight resistant, it varies from 1 to 6 feet high and much broader. Low forms are good for massing and ground cover. It is native to the mountains of central and southern Europe. 'Arcadia' is a ground cover just over 1 foot high, with bright green foliage. 'Broadmoor' is a low, form about 1 to 2 feet high and 6 feet wide, with bright green, fine-textured foliage. 'Skandia' is similar to 'Broadmoor' but with feathery, needle-like blue-green foliage.

J. scopulorum (Rocky Mountain juniper; 8' zones 4 to 8) has an upright growth habit, to 10 to 20 feet tall, and silvery to blue-green foliage. Cultivars are useful for vertical accent, hedges, screens, and windbreaks. It is native to dry ridges of the higher elevations of the Rocky Mountains from Alberta to Texas. 'Skyrocket' is narrowly columnar and slow-growing, eventually reaching about 12 feet tall. It has silvery blue foliage.

J. squamata (singleseed juniper; zones 4 to 7) was known for many years 6' only as the shapeless 'Meyeri'. Now represented by new cultivars, this species is reputedly not as heat tolerant as other junipers. It is native to China. 'Blue Star' is a dwarf that forms a mound 2 to 3 feet high and 5 to 6 feet wide, with blue needles and yellow-tipped blue-green scale like foliage. It grows like a smaller version of J. × media 'Pfitzeriana'.

Juniperus sabina *'Blue Forest'*

Juniperus scopulorum *'Skyrocket'*

Juniperus scopulorum *'Silver King'*

Juniperus squamata *'Blue Star'*

Juniperus virginiana *'Nova'*

Juniperus virginiana *'Grey Owl'*

Two of the many exciting new introductions in mountain laurel. Above: 'Ostbo Red'; inset: 'Carousel'

KALMIA LATIFOLIA

KAL-mee-a la-ti-FOH-lee-a

Mountain laurel

9'
7'
- Dense, rounded habit
- Not a good choice for dry gardens
- Flowers in clusters
- Zones 5 to 8

This eastern U.S. woodland native has spectacular white to deep pink flowers and evergreen foliage; medium textured, it becomes gnarled and open in old age. It is considered one of the finest of all American native shrubs.

USE: Use it as a specimen or as a companion for azaleas and rhododendrons. Growth rate: slow.
CULTURE: Grow it in acidic, cool, moist soil high in organic matter, in full or half sun.
RECOMMENDED CULTIVARS:
Increasing numbers of excellent cultivars are becoming available, mostly due to the work of Dr. Richard Jaynes of the Connecticut Agricultural Experiment Station. 'Sarah' has red buds that open brilliant pinkish red, and a compact habit. 'Elf' is a dwarf with pink buds opening white. 'Ostbo Red' has red buds that open lighter pink. 'Raspberry Glow' has maroon buds opening deep raspberry-pink.

Kerria japonica 'Variegata (above) imparts a glow to woodlands even when not in bloom. Inset: 'Pleniflora'

KERRIA JAPONICA

CARE-i-a ja-PON-i-ca

Kerria

7'
10'
- Bright yellowspring flowers
- Bright green stems
- Good in shade
- Zones 5 to 9

A tough, carefree, shade plant, its stems provide winter color in winter. Native to western and central China.
USE: Use in borders, masses, groups, and where shade is an opportunity. Combine kerria with *Mahonia aquifolium* and *Adiantum*

pedatum. Growth rate: slow to establish, fast when established.
CULTURE: Plant in light to half shade because flowers fade in full sun. Plant in a protected location with good drainage to reduce the chance of winter damage. Prune directly after flowering, since it flowers on last year's growth.
RECOMMENDED CULTIVARS:
'Pleniflora' is double-flowered and showy. 'Variegata' (also known as 'Picta') has white-variegated foliage and slower growth. It is unstable, developing green-leaved shoots that must be cut out. 'Shannon' and 'Golden Guinea' have single flowers 1½ to 2 inches in diameter.

Beautybush is an old-fashioned favorite for spectacular late spring bloom.

KOLKWITZIA AMABILIS

kole-KWIT-zee-a ah-MAH-bi-lis

Beautybush

10'
10'
- Low-maintenance
- Profuse pale pink flowers
- Medium texture in summer
- Zones 5 to 8

This shrub has limited value when not in flower; it has light-brown, somewhat ragged peeling bark on lower trunks. Native to central China.

USE: Best used in the rear of the shrub border in large gardens. Good companion plants include *Berberis thunbergii* 'Crimson Pygmy' and *Lamium maculatum* 'Beacon Silver'. Growth rate: fast.
CULTURE: Indifferent to soil type or pH. Give it a sunny location and plenty of room to grow. Prune out older stems every year after flowering; it flowers on old wood. Renew by cutting to the ground.
RECOMMENDED CULTIVARS:
'Pink Cloud' and 'Rosea' have deeper pink flowers.

LAGERSTROEMIA INDICA

lay-ger-STREE-mee-a IN-di-ka

Crape myrtle

8'

8'

- Red, pink, white, or lavender flowers
- Spectacular in fall
- Mottled winter bark
- Zones 7 to 9

This shrub or small tree makes an outstanding all-season plant. It blooms midsummer to early fall. New spring leaves are bronze. Native to China and Korea.

USE: A handsome specimen underplanted with a ground cover, it also can be used as a foundation planting, a hedge, or screen. Plant it with *Osmanthus heterophyllus* and *Vinca major*. Growth rate: fast.

CULTURE: Plant in moist, well-drained soil rich in organic matter and in hot sun. Grow only mildew-resistant varieties. Prune annually to increase flowering by removing spent flower clusters and twiggy growth on small shrubs, or 12 to 18 inches of each branch on large ones. (Never cut a branch under an old fruit cluster larger than a small finger.)

RECOMMENDED CULTIVARS: While many varieties are trees to 25 feet tall, dozens of good shrub-sized cultivars are available in sizes from 2 to 8 feet tall, with strong, variable bark interest and autumn foliage color. 'Centennial' has purple flowers, 'Hopi' and 'Pecos' pink, 'Tonto' red and 'Acoma' white.

Crape myrtle is unbeatable for showy summer flowers and fall foliage. Winter bark is lovely, too.

LAVANDULA ANGUSTIFOLIA

la-VAN-dew-la an-goose-ti-FOH-li-a

English lavender

1'

3'

- Evergreen
- Fragrant lavender-purple flower spikes early to late summer
- Scented leaves
- Zones 5 to 8

Cultivated for centuries for its fragrance and beauty, lavender has silvery or bluish green leaves, a fine texture, and mounded habit. Native to the Mediterranean region.

USE: Use it in perennial or shrub borders or as a low hedge in a parterre or herb garden. Companions include sage, thyme, dwarf boxwood, and germander cultivars. Growth rate: slow.

CULTURE: Give it a well-drained, rather dry spot in the garden with neutral to alkaline pH. Prune off flower stalks after they've bloomed. Overwatering kills lavender.

RECOMMENDED CULTIVARS: 'Hidcote' has deep purple flowers and silver leaves; it grows to 12 inches tall. 'Munstead' has lilac spikes and gray-green leaves; it reaches 18 inches tall. 'Nana' has lavender-purple flowers and is reputed to be more cold hardy. 'Rosea' has soft pink flowers.

English lavender 'Hidcote' bears especially intense, dark purple flowers in early summer.

LEPTOSPERMUM SCOPARIUM

lep-toh-SPER-mum sco-PAR-ee-um

New Zealand tea-tree

10'

10'

- Evergreen
- Good for West Coast
- Red, pink, or white flowers
- Zones 9 to 10

This versatile plant with fragrant, fine-textured, narrow leaves varies from a shrub 10 feet tall to an 8-inch ground cover. Tea-tree blooms profusely from late winter to midsummer. Native to New Zealand.

USE: It can serve as a specimen, accent, or focal point in coastal shrub borders. Prostrate forms make colorful ground covers but do not suppress weeds. Use it with *Rosmarinus officinalis* 'Prostratus' and *Hebe*. Growth rate: medium.

CULTURE: Needs thorough drainage and full sun. It is drought tolerant and pest free once established. Shear or prune lightly for a formal appearance. Never prune into bare wood, which prevents buds from breaking into new growth.

RECOMMENDED CULTIVARS: 'Gaiety Girl' has double, salmon-pink flowers. 'Red Damask' produces double, cherry-red flowers on a dense shrub 6 to 8 feet high.

New Zealand tea is a must for the coastal West. Above: 'Pom Pom'; inset: 'Sunraysia'

'Girard's Rainbow' is a cultivar of drooping leucothoe with attractive multi-colored foliage.

LEUCOTHOË FONTANESIANA

lu-KOH-tho-ee fon-ta-nee-see-AN-a

Drooping leucothoe

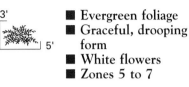
3'   5'

- Evergreen foliage
- Graceful, drooping form
- White flowers
- Zones 5 to 7

Leucothoe makes a fine companion for rhododendrons, azaleas, and mountain laurels. Native to mountain streamsides from Virginia to Tennessee.

USE: Naturalize it in a shady woodland garden, or use it as a foreground plant for leggy shrubs, as a graceful, ground cover for shady slopes, or in the shrub border. Its cascading form is lovely hanging over a wall. Growth rate: slow to moderate.

CULTURE: Plant it in acid, moist, well-drained soil high in organic matter. It needs full shade, ample moisture, and protection from drought and drying winds. Prune after flowering. Rejuvenate by cutting to the ground.

RECOMMENDED CULTIVARS: 'Girard's Rainbow' has yellow, green, and copper-variegated foliage. 'Nana' is a dwarf form.

LIGUSTRUM

li-GUS-trum

Privet

10'   6'

- Low maintenance, evergreen or deciduous
- Strongly scented white flowers
- Lustrous leaves
- Zones vary with species

Highly adaptable and trouble-free, privet responds well to pruning and shaping.

USE: Used most often as formal or informal hedges, backgrounds, and screens. Use privet with *Hedera helix* and *Chrysogonum virginianum*. Growth rate: fast.

CULTURE: Adaptable to most soils in sun to partial shade. For flowers,

Border privet is a classic choice for hedges in the North and Midwest. Inset: L. ovalifolium 'Aureum'

prune just after it blooms in early summer. Otherwise, prune any time.

RECOMMENDED CULTIVARS AND RELATED SPECIES: *L. japonicum* (zones 7 to 10) is an evergreen 6 to 12 feet high with compact, tight habit and wavy leaves. *L.* 'Vicaryi' (golden privet, Zones 5 to 8) is a deciduous shrub with yellow-green leaves. *L. obtusifolium* (border privet; zones 4 to 8) has deciduous foliage and horizontal growth habit. *L. ovalifolium* (California privet; zones 6 to 10) is a popular, semievergreen hedge plant. *L. vulgare* (common privet, zones 5 to 10) is a plant to avoid, very susceptible to anthracnose.

'Compacta' is an especially dense form of Oregon grapeholly. Shown here in spring bloom.

MAHONIA AQUIFOLIUM

ma-HOH-nee-a a-kwi-FOH-lee-um

Oregon grapeholly

3'   4'

- Open, loose form
- Showy, bright yellow flowers in late April
- Spiny evergreen leaves
- Zones 5 to 9

A popular hardy evergreen for shady areas, its holly-like leaves turn purplish in cold weather. Yellow spring flowers are followed by purple fruits. Native to damp forests from British Columbia to Oregon.

USE: Best integrated into a shrub border or foundation planting, or as a specimen. Combine with *Hosta* and *Pachysandra*. Growth rate: slow.

CULTURE: Plant in moist acid soil and protect from hot sun and wind. Winter wind especially can dessicate and "burn" foliage, turning it brown, especially where snow cover is light. Prune annually after flowering to maintain a 3-foot height.

RECOMMENDED CULTIVARS AND RELATED SPECIES: 'Compacta' remains under 2 feet with little or no pruning. *M. repens* (creeping mahonia) has blue-green foliage and tolerates dry soil.

MAHONIA BEALEI

ma-HOH-nee-a BAY-lee-eye

Leatherleaf mahonia

7' / 6'

- Vertical stems
- Large clusters of yellow flowers
- Grape-like fruit
- Zones 6 (south) to 10

Striking structural interest makes this plant worth growing. Native to China.

USE: Leatherleaf mahonia has an exotic, tropical effect when displayed against a wall or lit dramatically at night. Use it with deciduous azaleas and *Convallaria majalis*. It makes an excellent container plant. Growth rate: slow.

CULTURE: Plant in rich, moist soil and give it plenty of water. Consider its ultimate size before planting because it is difficult to prune correctly. Avoid planting it where spiny foliage can scratch.

RELATED SPECIES: M. *lomariifolia* (Burmese mahnoia; zones 8 to 10) grows to 10 feet or more high, if allowed. It's tropical-looking, two-foot leaves have 20 to 40 leaflets, showy flowers and powdery blue fruit in clusters of 15 to 20.

Showy blue fruits and large, tropical-looking leaves are the hallmarks of leatherleaf mahonia.

MYRICA PENSYLVANICA

MIR-ih-ka pen-sil-VAN-i-ka

Northern bayberry

8' / 8'

- Aromatic
- White fruits all winter
- Deciduous foliage
- Zones 2 to 7

Valued for centuries for its fragrant berries, bayberry fixes its own nitrogen from the atmosphere and thus can grow in the poorest soils. Native to the coastal areas of the eastern U.S. and Great Lakes.

USE: Excellent for large-scale massing in poor soil, difficult urban sites, and coastal areas. Also good for the shrub border or informal hedge or for combining with broad-leaved evergreens. Companion plants include *Rosa virginiana* and *Juniperus conferta*. Growth rate: medium from old growth, fast from root suckers.

CULTURE: Plant in any soil in full sun to partial shade, but it prefers dry infertile, sandy soil. Pest free, it is tolerant of salt spray and wind. Prune to renew branches and renew old leggy plants by pruning to the ground.

RELATED SPECIES: M. *cerifera* (wax myrtle) grows to 10 to 15 feet tall, making a fine specimen shrub or small tree, in zones 7 to 10.

A must for naturalistic seaside plantings, northern bayberry has a refined, almost layered habit.

MYRTUS COMMUNIS

MUR-tus co-MYOON-nis

Myrtle

10' / 6'

- Evergreen leaves are fragrant when bruised
- Sweet-scented flowers
- Smooth, tan bark
- Zones 9 to 10

Commonly grown in hot, dry areas of Arizona and the coastal gardens of California, this is a wide, round, bushy shrub that bears white flowers in summer and has lustrous, dark green leaves. It is native to the Mediterranean region.

USE: Formal and informal hedges, screens, masses, or backgrounds. Plant it with *Lantana* species and *Nerium oleander*. Growth rate: moderate.

CULTURE: Myrtle grows in any soil with fast drainage. Best in full sun to partial shade. It shears well and is easily trained into a formal hedge.

RECOMMENDED CULTIVARS: 'Compacta' is slow growing and compact, to 3 feet tall. 'Variegata' has small white-margined leaves and is similar in size to 'Compacta'.

Superb for formal hedges in dry, mild climates, myrtle bears small white flowers in summer.

NANDINA DOMESTICA

nan-DEE-na do-MESS-ti-ka

Heavenly bamboo

Not actually a bamboo, heavenly bamboo bears striking fruits in fall. Inset: deep fall color of 'Gulf Stream'.

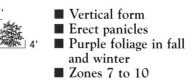

7'
4'

- Vertical form
- Erect panicles
- Purple foliage in fall and winter
- Zones 7 to 10

Popular in southern gardens for its ornamental assets and easy care, its creamy white flowers are borne on the ends of vertical branches in June, followed by bright red clusters of berries. Its vertical form contrasts with wispy foliage that is evergreen in mild climates and dies back elsewhere. Native to China and Japan.

USE: Heavenly bamboo is effective in a mass, as a specimen, or in a container. Use it with *Ilex* species and *Begonia grandis*. Growth rate: moderate.

CULTURE: Grow heavenly bamboo in nearly any soil in sun or shade, but it requires protection in hot climates. It is drought tolerant when established. Use it as a herbaceous perennial in the North. Plant heavenly bamboo in groups because cross-fertilization improves fruiting. Prune out leggy canes annually to increase density. Exhibits chlorosis (yellowing) in alkaline soils.

RECOMMENDED CULTIVARS: 'Harbour Dwarf' grows into a dense 2- to 3-foot-high mound with purplish winter color. 'Gulf Stream' is a robust, compact mound 2 to 3 feet high with red winter color.

NERIUM OLEANDER

NEAR-ee-um OH-lee-an-der

Oleander

So easy and tough it's a freeway plant in California, oleander bears showy flowers nearly all summer.

15'
15'

- Coarse evergreen foliage
- Red, pink, white, or yellow flowers
- Broad, round habit
- Zones 8 to 10

A no-fuss, drought-tolerant shrub that is very popular west of the Rockies and in the South, Oleander is native to the Mediterranean region. All parts of this plant are poisonous.

USE: Excellent for desert gardens and California. Plant with *Ceanothus* species, *Raphiolepsis indica*, and *Escallonia* varieties. Growth rate: fast.

CULTURE: Plant it in full sun, in any soil from dry sand to wet clay. It tolerates heat, salt, and drought. In shady or humid environments, it's prone to mildew, scale, aphids, and many other insects and diseases. Prune in early spring to control size and form. Remove old wood that has flowered each year. Tip-pinch to encourage density, or pull off suckers from the base to encourage more open height. Be extremely cautious with clippings from pruning. Smoke from burning plant parts can cause severe skin and respiratory irritations. Contact with leaves can cause dermatitis. Ingesting even small amounts can cause severe illness or death.

OSMANTHUS FRAGRANS

oz-MAN-thus FRAY-grans

Sweet olive

Hardly any flower is more fragrant than sweet olive (above). Inset, left: holly osmanthus 'Variegatus'.

15'
10'

- Powerfully fragrant, nearly year-round flowers
- Evergreen foliage
- Neat, compact habit
- Zones 8 to 10

Native to eastern Asia.

USE: Outstanding hedge, screen, background, espalier, or container plant. Combine it with *Pittosporum tobira* and *Ceratostigma plumbaginoides*. Growth rate: moderate.

CULTURE: Plant it in any soil from sand to clay. Keep it low by shearing. Prune any time of year. Pinch growing tips to encourage denseness.

RECOMMENDED CULTIVARS AND RELATED SPECIES: 'Aurantiacus' has fragrant orange blossoms mostly in October. *O. delavayi* (Delavay osmanthus; zones 8 to 10) has finely textured leaves, graceful arching habit, and large white flowers that are profuse and fragrant from late March to May. It's handsome on banks and walls where branches can cascade. *O. heterophyllus* (holly osmanthus; zones 7 to 10), often confused with English holly, has lustrous, spiny, dark green leaves and fragrant, hidden, cream-colored flowers in the fall; it is unusually shade tolerant. 'Variegatus' has cream-colored leaf margins.

PAEONIA SUFFRUTICOSA

pee-OH-nee-a suf-fru-ti-KOH-sa

Tree peony

4'
4'
- Enormous flowers last up to 10 days
- 18-inch leaves
- Open leggy habit
- Zones 5 to 9

Although its deciduous foliage is attractive, this shrub is chiefly grown for its immense blooms in red, green, pink, purple, maroon, white, blue, or multicolors. Native from Bhutan to Tibet and China.
USE: Plant with *Clethra* and Siberian iris. Growth rate: slow.

CULTURE: Plant in early fall in well-drained, moist, rich soil amended with ample organic matter. Locate carefully in full sun to light shade because it does not transplant well. Plant grafted forms with the graft union at least 4 inches below the ground to encourage the grafts to form their own roots. Protect from rabbits during the first year and mulch well. Don't mulch after the first year, and remove faded blossoms immediately to help control botrytis fungus. Largest flowers may need staking.
RECOMMENDED CULTIVARS: There are many cultivars to select from for flower color and form.

Above: red 'Thunderbolt' and yellow 'Amber Moon' tree peonies. Inset, right: 'Yae Zakura'.

PHILADELPHUS CORONARIUS

fil-a-DEL-fus co-ro-NAH-ree-us

Sweet mockorange

00'
6'
5'
- Deliciously fragrant, flowers in late spring
- Coarse textured
- Leggy, straggly habit
- Zones 4 to 8

This shrub is popular for sweet-scented flowers. Native to Europe and southwestern Asia.
USE: Grow it where you can smell it—in the border, near outdoor living areas, entryways, and windows. Companion plants include *Aquilegia* species and *Pachysandra terminalis*. Growth rate: fast.
CULTURE: Easy to grow and pest free, mockorange is not particular about soil; it takes sun or partial shade. Prune annually right after flowering by removing older wood or cutting to the ground. Buy plants when in flower to determine fragrance.
RELATED SPECIES: Hybrids: 'Miniature Snowflake' ('Double Snowflake') grows to only 2 to 3 feet tall, with fragrant double white flowers. 'Galahad' grows to 5 feet tall and wide, with fragrant white flowers. 'Minnesota Snowflake' is fragrant, grows 6 feet high, and is hardy to zone 4.

Sweet mockorange is famed for fragrance in late spring and early summer. Inset: 'Aureus'

PHOTINIA X FRASERI

fo-TIN-ee-uh FRAY-zer-eye

Redtip photinia

20'
18'
- Bronze-red new foliage
- Ivory flowers
- Red berries attractive to birds
- Zones 7 to 10

Popular in southern gardens for its lustrous, red-tipped leaves in spring, it produces malodorous flowers in clusters in late March and April. Hybrid origin.
USE: Use it as a screen, hedge, or single-trunked small tree. Combine it with *Nerium oleander* and *Cistus* species. Growth rate: moderate to fast.
CULTURE: Plant in well-drained soil amply amended with organic matter. Even though it is heat resistant, water it generously, without splashing water on the leaves; foliage is susceptible to fire blight, which blackens the branch ends. Prune out diseased branches, sterilizing the shears in alcohol or bleach after each cut, and destroy the refuse.
RELATED SPECIES: *P. serratifolia* (Chinese photinia; zones 7 to 10).

Redtip photinea is a much-used shrub for tall hedges and screens in the South.

PICEA ABIES 'NIDIFORMIS'

pie-SEE-a AY-bees ni-di-FOR-mis

Bird's-nest spruce

Bird's-nest spruce (right) and dwarf Alberta spruce (left) are two of the most popular dwarf conifers.

3' / 6'
- Dwarf conifer
- Often indented in the center like a bird's nest
- Finely textured, needled foliage
- Zones 2 to 5

A versatile and popular dwarf spruce for the North. Native to northern and central Europe.
USE: Combine it with *Pinus mugo* ssp. *mugo* and *Juniperus horizontalis*. Growth rate: slow.
CULTURE: It prefers full sun to light shade in well-drained, sandy, moderately moist soil, but tolerates other soils as long as they are moist. It also prefers deep winter cold and cool summers. Avoid hot, dry sites.

Harmed by urban pollution.
RELATED SPECIES: There are numerous dwarf cultivars of different species of spruces that are useful as shrub-like masses. *P. glauca* 'Conica' (dwarf Alberta spruce; zones 2 to 7) is stiffly and densely conical. A slow-growing dwarf conifer, it reaches 6 to 8 feet in 50 years. *Picea pungens* 'Montgomery' forms a broad cone only 6 feet high after many years, with beautiful silvery blue foliage. *Picea pungens* 'Glauca Globosa' is a rounded dwarf with silvery foliage, reaching only 3 to 4 feet after many years.

PIERIS JAPONICA

pee-AIR-is ja-PON-i-ka

Japanese andromeda

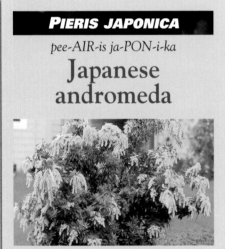

'Forest flame' Japanese andromeda in bloom (above) and after bloom (near right). Far right: 'Pink Flamingo'

7' / 6'
- Upright habit
- Delicate, pinkish white panicles
- Colorful new growth
- Zones 6 to 9

This broad-leaved evergreen blooms in early spring for 2 to 3 weeks and is attractive year-round. Native to Japan.
USE: Use as a specimen, in the shrub border, or combine with other acid-loving broad-leaved evergreens, including *Ilex* species and *Leucothoë fontanesiana*. Growth rate: slow.
CULTURE: Plant andromeda in moist, acid soil, protected from wind and winter sun, especially in zones 6 and 7. It seldom needs

pruning. It sometimes has insect and mite problems.
RECOMMENDED CULTIVARS AND RELATED SPECIES: There are many good cultivars selected for colorful new spring growth, flower color, and overall form and size. 'Dorothy Wycoff' has dark red buds that open to pale pink flowers. *P. floribunda* (mountain andromeda; zones 5 to 8) is hardier and lower than *P. japonica*.

PINUS MUGO SPP. MUGO

pie-nus MEW-go

Dwarf mountain pine

Take care to select reliably dwarf varieties of mugo pine. 'Carston's Gold' (inset) has luminous foliage.

16' / 20'
- Dark-needled evergreen
- Bushy, spreading habit
- Medium texture
- Zones 2 to 8, except for the desert

Bought as a small cushion, it becomes a very big bush. Native to the mountains of Europe from Spain to the Balkans.
USE: Use it for textural evergreen interest in a foundation planting, as low masses, or in groupings. Plant it with *Rhododendron canadense* and *Arctostaphylos uva-ursi*. Growth rate: slow.
CULTURE: Plant in moist, deep

loam in full sun to part shade. To maintain a compact, dense form, prune annually by removing two-thirds of each young, expanding candle in the spring. Be sure to grow truly dwarf cultivars if you want a plant less than 15 tall and wide.
RECOMMENDED CULTIVARS AND RELATED SPECIES: *Pinus mugo* ssp. *mugo* is the commonly sold variety; it can eventually reach 16 feet high and 20 feet wide. 'Enci', 'Gnome', and 'Mops' are reliably small cultivars. *P. strobus* 'Nana' (dwarf eastern white pine; zones 3 to 8) and *P. sylvestris* 'Beuvronensis' (dwarf Scotch pine; zones 2 to 8) are a few of the many dwarf cultivars of other pines.

PITTOSPORUM TOBIRA

pit-o-SPOH-rum to-BEER-ra

Japanese pittosporum

5'
6'

- Leathery leaves
- Rich fragrance in bloom
- Broad, dense habit
- Zones 8 south to 10

Pleasing foliage and creamy yellow spring flowers make this a popular plant in southern and western gardens. Native to Japan and China.

USE: It's good for screens, massing, and in borders, and is effective in containers or trained as small, crooked-stemmed trees. Plant it with *Punica granatum* and *Pyracantha coccinea*. Growth rate: slow.

CULTURE: Prefers full sun to partial shade but tolerates deep shade. Fairly drought resistant, but water as needed during drought.

RECOMMENDED CULTIVARS AND RELATED SPECIES: 'Variegata' has white-variegated gray-green foliage and grows to about 5 feet high. 'Wheeler's Dwarf' grows only to about 2 feet in many years. *P. crassifolium* (zones 9 to 10) is a large shrub up to 25 feet high

that can form a dense hedge 6 feet high. Fine-textured gray-green leaves respond well to shearing and tolerate wind and salt. 'Nana' is a dwarf 3 feet high.

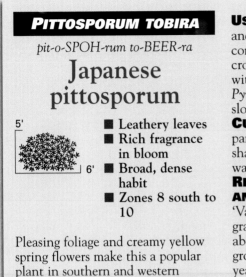

'Wheeler's Dwarf' Japanese pittosporum (above) remains a small cushion. Inset: 'Variegata'.

PLATYCLADUS ORIENTALIS (FORMERLY THUJA ORIENTALIS)

pla-tee-CLA-dus o-ree-en-TAL-is

Oriental arborvitae

8'
5'

- Tall evergreen conifer
- Branches in vertical, fan-shaped planes
- Available with bright yellow or blue foliage
- Zones 7 to 9

Popular in the South and West for its blue and yellow dwarf cultivars. Native to China and Korea.

USE: In masses or groupings, or for textural evergreen interest in a foundation planting. Combine it with *Prunus laurocerasus* 'Otto Luyken' and *Chamaecyparis pisifera* 'Filifera Aurea'. Growth rate: slow to moderate.

CULTURE: It grows in all but wet soils and tolerates dry soil and atmosphere. Protect it from harsh dry winds.

RECOMMENDED CULTIVARS: 'Aurea Nana' is a rounded yellow dwarf, 2 to 3 feet tall. 'Blue Cone' is a pyramidal form that can grow to 8 feet tall with blue-green needles.

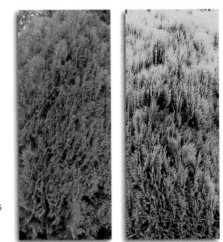

The emerald green foliage of Oriental arborvitae (left), and the glowing golden leaves of 'Aurea Nana' (right).

POTENTILLA FRUTICOSA

po-ten-TIL-la fru-ti-COH-sa

Bush-cinquefoil

3'
3'

- Neat, rounded habit
- Prolific, bright summer flowers
- Deciduous foliage
- Zones 3 to 7

A small, versatile shrub for most conditions. Native to meadows and bogs of northern and mountainous Asia, Europe, and North America.

USE: Suitable for shrub borders, foundations, massing, edging, informal low hedges, or facing down larger shrubs. Use it with *Rosa*

rugosa and *Euonymus alatus* 'Compactus'. Growth rate: slow.

CULTURE: It tolerates most well-drained soils and extreme cold and drought. It is susceptible to mites. Flowers best in full sun but tolerates partial shade. Plant orange-and-red-flowering varieties in partial shade because they fade in full sun.

RECOMMENDED CULTIVARS AND RELATED SPECIES: 'Abbotswood' produces large white flowers on a spreading shrub. 'Goldfinger' is one of the best for bright yellow flowers. 'Primrose Beauty' has pale yellow flowers and silvery leaves. *P. atrosanguinea* 'Gibson's Scarlet' produces profuse red flowers.

Top: 'Abbotswood' bush-cinquefoil. Bottom left: 'Red Ace'; bottom right: 'Gold Star'.

'Otto Luyken' is a dwarf form of evergreen cherry laurel that only reaches 3 to 4 feet high.

PRUNUS LAUROCERASUS

PROO-nus lohr-o-ser-ASS-sus

Cherry laurel

20'
18'

- Large dark evergreen leaves
- Large shrub or small tree
- Medium texture
- Zones 7 to 8

Cherry laurel is a popular hedge plant in southern gardens and in California. Unpruned it can grow into a small tree or large shrub 20 feet high.

USE: It makes a handsome formal hedge, screen, or background plant.

Growth rate: medium.

CULTURE: Plant in any soil in partial shade. Prune it selectively and frequently because it grows fast and shearing mutilates the large leaves. Beware of its greedy, far-reaching roots.

RECOMMENDED CULTIVARS: A number of smaller cultivars are available that are quite restrained in habit and size. Schipkaensis' has smaller leaves, grows 4 to 5 feet tall, and is hardy to zone 6 with protection. 'Otto Luyken' is a low-growing form hardy to southern zone 6 that reaches only 3 to 4 feet high after many years. It is also hardier, surviving winters in zone 6.

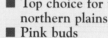

Nanking cherry (above) is a must for the harsh-winter plains states. Inset, left: Prunus 'Hally Jolivette'.

PRUNUS TOMENTOSA

PROO-nus toh-men-TOH-sa

Nanking cherry

9'
15'

- Open, spreading, twiggy habit
- Top choice for the northern plains
- Pink buds
- Zones 2 to 7

Valuable for its extreme hardiness, fragrant white or pink spring flowers, and delicious scarlet fruit. Native to the Himalayas.

USE: Good for a specimen, hedge, in groups and masses, or in a shrub border. It's attractive with *Ilex*

glabra, Chaenomeles speciosa and *Caragana arborescens*. Growth rate: medium.

CULTURE: Plant in any soil in partial shade.

RELATED SPECIES AND HYBRIDS: 'Hally Jolivette' (a hybrid between Higan cherry and *Prunus × yedoensis*; zones 5 to 8) is an airy shrub or small tree with pink-eyed white flowers that open over 3 weeks. *P. × cistena* (purple-leaf sand cherry; zones 4 to 7) is valued for extreme hardiness and white flowers against reddish-purple leaves. *P. triloba* f. *multiplex* (flowering almond; zones 6 to 9) is a large, tree-like shrub 12 to 15 feet high with small pink double flowers.

'Nana' is a dwarf pomegranate with perfectly proportioned, small flowers and fruit. Inset: bloom detail.

PUNICA GRANATUM

PEW-ni-ka gra-NAY-tum

Pomegranate

15'
15'

- Red-orange flowers
- Delicious fruit
- Brilliant yellow autumn foliage
- Dense, twiggy, fountain-like
- Zones 8 to 10

An excellent desert shrub, it withstands heat, drought, and alkaline soils. A favorite landscape plant for California gardens. Native to southeastern Europe across Asia to the Himalayas.

USE: Selections for size range from container or edging plants to border shrubs 15 feet tall. The dwarf varieties make excellent low hedges. Plant it with *Callistemon citrinus* and *Cistus* species. Growth rate: moderate.

CULTURE: Plant in full sun for best flowers and fruit. Water regularly for best fruit.

RECOMMENDED CULTIVARS: 'Wonderful' is the most popular form for fruit; it grows 8 to 12 feet tall. 'Nana' may grow to only 2 to 3 feet tall, with small flowers and tiny fruits in good proportion to its diminutive stature. It is also a good selection for growing in containers, and will flower and fruit indoors.

PYRACANTHA COCCINEA

pie-ra-KAN-tha kok-SIN-ee-a

Scarlet firethorn

10'
12'

- White spring flowers
- Red or orange fruit
- Upright to prostrate
- Zones 6 to 9, some cultivars to Zone 5

An easy-to-grow shrub for all seasons, it has evergreen foliage (semideciduous in the North).
USE: Useful as a specimen, barrier, or espaliered against walls and fences. Avoid planting next to path, entrance, or garage due to thorns. Growth rate: moderate to fast.

CULTURE: Grow in full sun and well-drained soil; don't move after established. Avoid standing water on foliage at bloomtime, as fire blight is a serious problem. Thorns make pruning difficult, so allow plenty of room to grow. Robins often become inebriated on fermented berries in early spring.
RECOMMENDED CULTIVARS: Many cultivars are available, bred for fruit color, form, hardiness, and disease resistance. 'Mohave', (zone 6), has orange-red fruit and is resistant to bird feeding, fire blight, and scab. 'Rutgers' (zone 6) grows 2 to 3 feet tall, has orange fruit, and resists scab and fire blight. 'Kasan' and 'Lalandei" are hardy to zone 5.

Scarlet firethorn 'Mohave' (above and inset) is resistant to bird feeding, fire blight, and scab.

RHAMNUS FRANGULA

RAM-nus FRANG-you-la

Glossy buckthorn

15'
4'

- Upright habit useful for hedge or screen
- Shiny dark leaves
- Fruit matures from red to purple to black
- Zones 2 to 7

The species is invasive and unexciting. 'Asplenifolia' has merit.
USE: The cultivar 'Columnaris' was a common hedge or screen in the Midwest until its disease-prone nature ended its use. Now *Rhamnus* is rarely used in the landscape.

Growth rate: moderate to fast.
CULTURE: Plant in well-drained soil in full sun to partial shade. This plant is highly susceptible to disease when under stress. It has become a serious woodland weed in the Midwest and Northeast.
RECOMMENDED CULTIVARS:
'Asplenifolia' has narrow, thread-like leaves with rough margins that curl on the stems of a 10- to 12-foot-high shrub. It is effective as a specimen, especially against a dark wall for contrast.

Once common as a hedge, glossy buckthorn can spread invasively by seed. One cultivar has merit.

RHAPHIOLEPIS INDICA

ra-fee-o-LEP-is IN-di-ka

Indian hawthorn

4'
5'

- Evergreen foliage
- Neat, dense habit
- Flowers bloom in spring, repeat in fall
- Zones 8 south to 10

Low-maintenance, restrained shrub has leathery foliage and white or red flowers and serves a multitude of purposes. Native to southern China.
USE: Indian hawthorn can be planted for low background, in a mass, in an informal hedge, or as a large-scale ground cover. Use it as a

foreground or a facing plant in a shrub border or as a container plant. Suitable companion plants include *Punica granatum* and *Coprosma repens*. Growth rate: slow.
CULTURE: It prefers full sun but tolerates partial shade and a variety of soils. Reasonably drought tolerant, it performs best when watered frequently. Minimize splashing water onto foliage, because fire blight and leaf spots can be problems.
RELATED SPECIES: *R. umbellata* (yedda hawthorn; zones 8 to 10) is a larger version of *R. indica*, growing to 5 to 6 feet high and wide. *R. ×delacourii* (hybrid Indian hawthorn) is intermediate between its parents,

the two species listed, and includes some of the best cultivars.

Indian hawthorn 'Enchantress' bears striking deep-rose flowers on low plants 3 feet high and 5 feet wide.

RHODODENDRON SPECIES

ro-do-DEN-dron

Rhododendrons and azaleas

- Beautiful flowers
- Rounded form
- Evergreen or deciduous foliage
- Zones 3 to 10, depending on species

Rhododendrons and azaleas differ in subtle ways, but all 900 species belong to the genus *Rhododendron*. Rhododendron flowers resemble bells, and azalea blossoms look like funnels. Most rhododendrons are evergreen, and most azaleas are deciduous. For convenience, we divided the genus into three groups: rhododendrons, evergreen azaleas, and deciduous azaleas.

USE: They are outstanding for shrub borders, woodland edges, foundation plantings, masses, groupings, and (for small species) in rock gardens. Rhododendrons look good with Kalmias, *Enkianthus*, hollies, other rhododendrons and azaleas, and ground covers such as *Adiantum pedatum* and *Epimedium* species. Growth rate: usually slow.

CULTURE: Plant in well-drained, acid soil. In the South, rhododendrons need more shade than in the North, where light shade is adequate. Keep them away from alkaline soil, salt spray, and harsh winter sun and wind.

Recommended evergreen rhododendrons:

R. carolinianum (Carolina rhododendron; zones 5 to 8) is a restrained, rounded shrub 3 to 6 feet high with white or pink flowers against dark, medium-size, evergreen leaves. Native to the Blue Ridge Mountains of the Carolinas and Tennessee.

R. catawbiense (catawba rhododendron; zones 4 to 7) grows 6 to 10 feet high and wide in the garden. It produces prolific trusses of reddish purple flowers against dark green leaves. Native to the Allegheny Mountains from West Virginia to Georgia and Alabama.

R. maximum (rosebay rhododendron; zones 4 to 7) reaches 4 to 15 feet high in the garden with a loose, open habit. Flowers are white or rosy purple. It needs at least partial shade to thrive. Native from North Carolina to Georgia and Alabama.

R. yakushimanum is compact, 3 feet high and wide, with white flowers. Dark green leaves have fuzzy undersides. 'Yaku Princess' has red to pink buds that open pure white; leaves are smooth underneath. Native to Japan.

R. yakushimanum *'Yaku Sunrise'*

'P.J.M. Compact'

R. catawbiense *'Album'*

'America'

'Meadowgold'

R. augustinii

'Scintillation'

'Blue Peter'

P.J.M. hybrids, hardy to zone 5, are rounded shrubs 3 to 6 feet tall. Dark green leaves turn purple in fall. Lavender-pink flowers last into autumn in the Southeast.

Dexter hybrids are big and hardy, and have dense leaves and beautiful flowers in yellows, pinks, and reds. 'Wheatley' bears yellow-blotched pink flowers on a shrub 6 feet tall and hardy to zone 5. 'Scintillation', a pink, is the most famous Dexter.

Old, popular ironclads include 'Boule de Neige', with glossy dark evergreen leaves, a compact rounded habit, and lovely white flower trusses. Hardy to northern zone 4, it is heat and sun tolerant.

RECOMMENDED EVERGREEN AZALEA HYBRIDS:

Southern Indian hybrids (Indian; zones 8 to 10) were developed for greenhouse forcing but now are a common landscape plant in southern and California

gardens. There are tender Belgian Indian hybrids and more vigorous and sun tolerant southern Indians. Flowers range from white to violet, pink, red, and salmon.

Kurume hybrids are Japanese hybrids popular in the landscape. Slow growing, they reach 6 feet tall and are hardy in zones 6 to 9.

Gable hybrids (zones 6 to 8) are bred for increased hardiness but should not be used north of zone 6. Their evergreen leaves redden and fall in the northern part of their range. They are mid-size shrubs with flowers in red to purple hues, with some light violets, orange-reds, and pinks available.

R. kaempferi (torch azaleas; zones 6 to 8) flower white to rose to red-orange and salmon on a shrub up to 10 feet tall. Foliage is semievergreen in the North, evergreen in the South, and often turns red in cold weather. It flowers

well in the deepest shade but prefers light shade.

Girard hybrids produce large, lovely flowers in pink, purple, white, and red on a handsome, evergreen shrub about 4 to 6 feet high. They are good for northern zones 6 to southern zone 9.

Glenn Dale hybrids are cold hardy in zones 6 south to 9 north, and grow 3 to 8 feet tall. They bloom from early to late season, with large, varied flowers in pink, red, orange-red, and white with flecks or stripes in a darker, contrasting color.

Robin Hill hybrids are hardy and reliable to about 10° F. They have big, late flowers up to 4 inches in diameter in pale pink, lavender, white, salmon, and red.

Shammarello hybrids, bred for cold climates, are hardy in zones 5 north to 9 south.

'Pink Jewel', Kurume hybrid azalea

'Hinode Giri', Kurume hybrid azalea

'Sherwood Orchid', Kurume hybrid azalea

'Coral Bells', Kurume hybrid azalea

'Laura Moorland', Robin Hill hybrid azalea

'Glacier', Glenn Dale hybrid azalea

'Fashion', Glenn Dale hybrid azalea

'Herbert', Glenn Dale hybrid azalea

RHODODENDRONS AND AZALEAS
continued

'Homebush', Knap Hill azalea

'Gibraltar', Exbury hybrid azalea

'Tutti Frutti', Exbury hybrid azalea

'Scarlet O'Hara', Exbury hybrid azalea

R. mucronulatum, *the Korean azalea, showing fall foliage*

R. mucronulatum, *spring bloom*

R. calendulaceum, *the flame azalea*

R. schlippenbachii, *royal azalea*

DECIDUOUS AZALEA HYBRIDS AND SPECIES are less particular about soil acidity and winter shade than evergreen varieties but are relatively intolerant of hot summer conditions:

Knap Hill-Exbury hybrids (zones 6 to 8, some hardy to zone 4) produce brilliant flowers in hundreds of colors. Blooms are large and borne in huge trusses. Medium green foliage turns vivid yellow, orange, and red in fall. They grow 4 to 8 feet high and wide.

R. arborescens (sweet azalea; zones 5 to 8) produces white flowers in early June and July with a fragrance similar to heliotrope. It grows 8 to 20 feet high and wide. Bright green summer leaves turn dark red in fall. Native to the East along mountain streams and in cool mountain meadows.

R. calendulaceum (flame azalea; zones 5 to 7) is native to the eastern U.S. Blooms range from yellow through orange and scarlet, and fiery fall foliage from yellow to bronze. Reaches 6 to 8 feet tall. Purchase this shrub in bloom because it's variable in color.

R. mucronulatum (Korean azalea, zones 5 to 8), blooms in very early spring with bright, rosy purple blooms that are sometimes nipped by late frosts. For this reason it is best planted where protected from winter sun. Lovely with forsythia.

R. periclymenoides (pinxterbloom azalea, zones 4 to 8) bears pinkish white, fragrant flowers in late April or early May. It has a low, neat habit, 4 to 6 feet wide and high. Foliage is bright green in summer. It thrives in full sun and dry, sandy rocky soils—a rare exception for the genus. Native from Maine to South Carolina.

R. schlippenbachii (royal azalea; zones 5 to 8) is an upright, rounded shrub 6 to 8 feet high with dark green summer leaves that turn a kaleidoscope of colors in fall. Bears fragrant, pale pink to white flowers in early- to mid-May. Buy in bloom to be certain of flower color. Native to Manchuria, Korea, and Japan.

ROOS TYE-fi-na

Staghorn sumac

- Excellent fall color in red, orange and yellow
- Red fruit
- Ferny foliage
- Zones 4 to 8

Exotic, almost tropical look in a hardy plant native to eastern North America. Outstanding fall color.
USE: A suckering spreading habit, 15 to 25 feet high, makes it good for massing in large open areas distant from the house. Plant it with *Rudbeckia fulgida* 'Goldsturm' and *Pennisetum alopecuriodes*. Growth rate: slow from old growth, fast from suckers.
CULTURE: Adaptable to all but standing water, sumac prefers good drainage. When necessary, renew it by cutting to the ground in late winter.

RELATED SPECIES: *R. aromatica* 'Gro-Low' (fragrant sumac; zones 3 to 9) has lustrous green leaves and spreads 2 feet high and up to 8 feet wide. It makes an effective ground cover with often showy but variable orange-red fall color. *R. copallina* (shining sumac, zones 5 to 8) is excellent for ornamental use, rarely exceeding 10 feet high in cultivation. A long-lived native of the eastern United States, it has

great fall color and interesting silhouettes. *R. glabra* (smooth sumac; zones 2 to 9) has brilliant red and yellow fall color and fuzzy large red fruit clusters. It is invasive but good for large areas, growing 10 to 15 feet high and much wider.

Staghorn sumac in summer, with attractive rust-colored fruits.

Staghorn sumac in its fall glory.

RYE-beez al-PIE-num

Alpine currant

- Upright, twiggy
- Fruit attracts birds
- Deciduous; little fall color
- Zones 2 to 7

This very hardy European native grows easily in the northern United States.
USE: Companions include *Aster × frikartii* 'Monch' and *Coreopsis verticillata* 'Zagreb'. Growth rate: Moderate.
CULTURE: It adapts to any soil in full sun to shade. Prune at any time.
RECOMMENDED CULTIVARS AND RELATED SPECIES: 'Green Mound' is a dense, compact form 2 feet high, 3 feet wide. *R. odoratum* (clove currant; zones 4 to 6) has yellow flowers that smell like cloves. *R. sanguineum* 'King Edward VII' (winter currant; zones 5 to 6) has red flowers, is a compact 5 to 6 feet tall, and is native to the West.

Currants are good subjects for formal and informal gardens alike. Above, left: Ribes sanguineum *'Apple Blossom'*. **Above, right:** Ribes alpinum *'Pumilum'*.

Ribes sanguineum *'King Edward'*

Ribes odoratum

ROSA SPECIES

ROH-za

Rose

- Beautiful, fragrant
- Thorny stems
- Various habits
- Zones 2 to 10, depending on species

Seductive scent and magnificent flowers in many colors and forms make roses a perpetually popular garden plant.

USE: Depending on the variety, use roses for informal hedges, climbers, ground covers, edging, specimens, or bedding plants. Roses are lovely with boxwood, clematis, lavender switchgrass, and other roses. Growth rate: fast.

CULTURE: Plant in well-drained, slightly acid soil generously amended with compost, and in full sun. Gardeners need to prune and feed roses according to the requirements of each variety.

RECOMMENDED CULTIVARS AND RELATED SPECIES: More than 100 species of wild roses and thousands of hybrids exist. Most of those roses fall into the following classes.

5'
3'
Hybrid teas and grandifloras: Hybrid teas, the most popular rose class, are often bred for a classic high-centered form and long stems. They typically require regular feeding, pruning, and spraying for pests and diseases. Grandifloras are similar to hybrid teas but bloom profusely. Rosarians invented the grandiflora class for the 'Queen Elizabeth' rose in 1954.

3'
4'
Floribundas: These shrubs result from breeding hybrid teas and polyantha roses. They have a bushy habit, with each stem producing many flowers. Although floribundas still need regular care, they have better disease resistance than hybrid teas and tend to be hardier. They are good for massing.

2'
2'
Miniatures: Perfect for containers, edging, parterres, ground covers, and low hedges, miniature rose bushes can stand less than 6 inches high or, for climbing varieties, up to 12 feet tall. Often prolific bloomers, miniatures have small leaves, slender canes, and flowers measuring on average 1 inch in diameter. Because they've been hybridized with other classes of rose, they are extremely varied in habit, flower size, and flower form.

'Tropicana', hybrid tea

'Peace', hybrid tea

'Queen Elizabeth', grandiflora

'Double Delight', hybrid tea

'Perfect Moment', hybrid tea

'Iceberg', floribunda

'Debut', miniature

'Mister Lincoln', hybrid tea

'Sweet Chariot', miniature

'Betty Prior', floribunda

'Europeana', floribunda

'Brass Band', floribunda

8'

10'

Species roses: These are wild roses that come true from seed. Species roses bear five-petaled or single flowers. Some species roses have exceptional hardiness and adaptability. *Rosa multiflora*, for example, has become a serious weed problem in many parts of North America. Lovely species roses include *R. carolina*, *R. virginiana*, *R. rugosa* (introduced), and *R. rubrifolia* (introduced).

6'

6'

Old garden roses: This class contains many of the roses depicted in historical paintings and fabrics. Divided into subgroups, it is comprised of alba, bourbon, centifolia or cabbage, china, damask, gallica, hybrid perpetual, hybrid spinosissima, moss, noisette, portland, and tea roses. Old roses, also known as antique roses, prevailed in the garden until 1867, when the first hybrid tea roses were created. Shades of pink and white dominate old garden roses, and one bloom can have from five to more than one hundred petals. Most old garden roses are exquisitely fragrant, hardy, and pest and disease resistant.

4'

6'

Classic shrub roses: These encompass several categories of roses developed in the nineteenth and twentieth centuries. Of varying heights, they tend to have bushy, spreading habits, and many are cold-hardy, robust, and floriferous. The choices seem endless. For instance, 'Sally Holmes', which bears profuse single white flowers, can grow 10 feet tall and be trained as a climber. 'Frau Dagmar Hartopp', a rugosa hybrid, stands out not only for its five-petaled flowers but also for its big shiny red hips. Meilland, the French rose breeders, introduced several shrub roses including the pink 'Bonica' and Meidiland® roses in pink, red, and white, which make excellent low hedges or ground covers. For hardiness, and pest and disease resistance, the prairie roses developed by the late Iowa State University professor Griffith J. Buck are hard to beat. Buck's 'Carefree Beauty' blooms heavily in June with scented, bright pink flowers that repeat later in the season.

'Madame Isaac Perriere', old garden rose

'Tuscany Superb', old garden rose (gallica)

'Zephirine Drouhin', classic shrub (climber)

'Madame Hardy', old garden rose

Rosa gallica officinalis (Rosa mundi), old garden rose (gallica)

'Frau Dagmar Hartopp', classic shrub (rugosa)

'Dortmund', classic shrub (Kordesii hybrid)

'Topaz Jewel', classic shrub (rugosa hybrid)

R. 'Bonica', shrub

R. 'Carefree Beauty', classic shrub

ROSE
continued

Modern shrub roses: For many years, the focus of rose breeding was on hybrid teas, floribundas, and hardy, repeat-blooming shrubs. Old garden roses with their luxuriant petals, soft colors, and romantic fragrances were set aside, principally because most of them flowered just once in the spring. In the 1960s, however, David Austin, a British nurseryman, began a hybridizing program that continues today. The result is a new class of roses, modern shrubs, which blend the lush form, color, and scent of old garden roses with the ability to flower again and again that prevails in contemporary roses. Romantica®, another strain of hybrid shrub roses, comes from Meilland, the French hybridizer. These compact bushy shrubs bear flowers with the form, color, and fragrance of old-fashioned roses but, unlike old roses, Romanticas flower repeatedly during the season. They typically stand 3 to 4 feet high, except for climbers such as 'Eden', 8 feet, or 'Polka', 10 to 12 feet.

Climbers and hedges: Climbing roses have long flexible canes that can be tied to arbors, walls, fences, posts, and trellises. Tall climbers look spectacular trained up tree trunks. With their canes raised off the ground, climbers take up little space, making them appropriate for even the smallest sunny gardens, if trained. Without being tied to a support, however, climbers have no means to grow vertically. Instead, they form either tall arching shrubs or sprawling mounds, depending on the variety. Climbers range from 7 to more than 20 feet tall. Hedge roses are tough and hardy, and bloom almost continuously. They create excellent low barriers and charming, informal borders for country garden rooms. Simplicity hedge roses, for example, mix well with perennials and come in pink, red, purple, and white.

'Graham Thomas', modern shrub

'Fair Bianca', modern shrub

'Constance Spry', modern shrub

'Abraham Darby', modern shrub

'Othello', modern shrub

'John Cabot', rugosa hybrid

'Blaze Improved', climber

'Joseph's Coat', climber

'Eden', modern shrub (climber)

ROSMARINUS OFFICINALIS

rows MARE-i-nus oh-fi-si-NAL-is

Rosemary

4'
6'

- Evergreen with fragrant, edible foliage
- Blue flowers
- Attracts birds, bees
- Zones 7 south to 10 (some hardy to zone 6)

A Mediterranean native with a bushy irregular habit that flourishes on the West Coast and in the heat and humidity of the Southeast. It flowers from fall to winter.

USE: Shears well, makes a good hedge, useful in the dry shrub border. Also a delicious kitchen herb. Plant it with *Caryopteris × clandonensis* and *Calamagrossis × acutiflora* 'Karl Foerster'. Growth rate: moderate.

CULTURE: Salt, heat, sun, infertile soil, and drought tolerant, rosemary can take any well-drained soil except a wet one. Plant in full sun only. Prune it for a low hedge.

Don't give it too much water or fertilizer.

RECOMMENDED CULTIVARS: 'Collingwood Ingram', 'Lockwood de Forest', and 'Tuscan Blue'—selected for bright blue flowers and, in the case of 'Lockwood de Forest', a prostrate habit.

'Irene' is a recent introduction of Rosemary with intense blue flowers and a low, mounding form. It is ideal for spilling over stone walls.

SALIX CAPREA

SAY-liks ka-PREE-a

Goat willow

20'
20'

- Soft male catkins 1 to 2 inches long
- Large shrub or small tree
- Medium texture
- Zones 4 to 8

This is a more attractive form of pussy willow (*S. discolor*, the true native pussywillow, is a disease prone and unattractive plant). Leaves are short. Native to Europe.

USE: Rear of the border, or specimen next to ponds or other large bodies of water. Combine it with *Iris pseudacorus* and *Hibiscus moscheutos*. Growth rate: fast.

CULTURE: Grows in moist soils, wet areas, and on banks of ponds and streams in full sun. Prune in summer or fall to preserve spring catkins. Force catkins for decorative use by bringing stems indoors in late winter and placing them in a vase in indirect light.

RECOMMENDED CULTIVARS AND RELATED SPECIES:
'Pendula' is female weeping form for ground cover or small tree. *Salix arenaria* (creeping willow; zones 4 to 9) is a useful hardy ground cover with silvery leaves. It forms a mat only one foot tall and fifteen feet wide or more. *S. purpurea* (purple osier willow; zones 3 to 6) has fine-textured foliage on a rounded shrub 8 to 10 feet high. *S. gracilistyla* var. '*Melanostachys*' (black pussywillow; zones 5 to 7) has purple-black winter stems and male catkins that open near-black and turn yellow. It grows 6 to 10 feet tall.

Salix arenaria is a silver-leaved ground cover only one foot tall that forms a mat 15 feet wide or more.

Goat willow is the most ornamental form of pussywillow. It grows quite large, up to 20 feet tall and wide.

SPIRAEA JAPONICA

spy-REE-ja-PON-i-ka

Japanese spirea

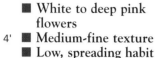

3'
4'

■ White to deep pink flowers
■ Medium-fine texture
■ Low, spreading habit
■ Zones 4 to 8

Flower clusters 6 inches wide appear over a long season June to August. **USE:** Spirea is good in masses and in the shrub border, where it makes a quick, easy-care filler, and where its dull, non-blooming appearance can be masked. Fine textured in summer, it is somewhat coarse in winter. Combine with *Pennisetum alopecuriodes* and *Imperata cylindrica*. Growth rate: fast.

CULTURE: Plant spirea in any soil in full sun and with good air circulation. Like all spireas, this species is susceptible to many pests and diseases, none of which is fatal. Because this spirea blooms on new growth, prune it in late winter or early spring. Cut old leggy plants to the ground in spring to renew them.

RECOMMENDED CULTIVARS AND RELATED SPECIES:
'Albiflora' has white and 'Anthony Waterer' has deep rose flowers. 'Crispa' grows 2 feet high with twisted leaves. 'Atrosanguinea' is a superior, deep rose-red cultivar 2 to 4 feet high and hardy to zone 4. 'Gold Flame' is low growing with brightly colored red, copper, and orange leaves in early spring and fall. 'Gold Mound' grows 2 feet high, has pink flowers; new foliage is bronze-red turning to golden yellow. 'Little Princess' is 2 feet high with fine-textured light green foliage and pink flowers. 'Shibori' is an upright mound to 3 feet high, with quantities of rose, pink and white flowers. *S. × vanhouttei* (Vanhoutte spirea) is a tough, fountain-like shrub 5 to 6 feet high and wide. White flowers appear on old growth in mid- to late-spring. *S. nipponica* var. *tosaensis* 'Snowmound' (snowmound spirea; zones 3 to 8) is a white-blooming species growing 3 to 5 feet high and wide. *S. prunifolia* var. *plena* (bridalwreath spirea; zones 4 to 8) is a rangy, open shrub, 4 to 9 feet high and 6 to 8 feet wide, with double white flowers in April on old growth. Leaves turn red-orange in autumn.

S. japonica *'Albiflora'*

S. japonica *'Shirobana'*

S. japonica *'Gold Flame'*

S. japonica *'Anthony Waterer'*

S. japonica *'Limemound'*

S. x vanhouttei, *(Vanhoutte spirea)*

S. × nipponica var. tosaensis 'Snowmound', *(snowmound spirea)*

S. prunifolia *(bridlewreath spirea)*

S. thunbergii *(thunberg spirea)*

SYRINGA VULGARIS

sur-RING-a vul-GARE-is

Common lilac

18'

15'

- Powerful floral fragrance
- Large conical flower clusters
- Bluish green foliage
- Zones 3 south to 7

Lilacs are valued in spring for their beauty and for the scent of their violet, purple, pink, blue, magenta, yellow, and white flowers. Native to southern Europe.

USE: Long-lived and capable of surviving most conditions, common lilac has an upright, irregular habit that's good in the back of the border. Plant it with *Berberis thunbergii* 'Atropurpurea' and *Viburnum dilatatum*. Growth rate: slow.

CULTURE: Plant in full sun in neutral, rich soil high in organic matter. Provide a location with good air circulation to help reduce problems with powdery mildew, to which these shrubs are susceptible. Some cultivars produce good flowers only every other year. Remove spent blossoms immediately to increase next year's flowering; prune out 50 to 75 percent of the basal suckers each year. Renew old plants by cutting them back almost to the ground.

RECOMMENDED CULTIVARS AND RELATED SPECIES:
Available cultivars number in the hundreds, selected mostly for color (white, pink, and shades of blue, lavender, violet, and purple). Most lilacs do best in cold climates. 'Lavender Lady', 'Blue Boy', 'Chiffon', 'Mrs. Forrest K. Smith', and 'Sylvan Beauty' do well in mild climates. *S. meyeri* 'Palibin' has pink flowers on a compact, floriferous, low-maintenance shrub. *S. patula* 'Miss Kim' is a tidy, blue-flowered oval shrub 6 to 8 feet high and 4 to 5 feet wide. *S. × persica* is a low shrub with smaller leaves and pale lavender, nearly scentless flowers.

'Macrostachya'

'Sensation'

'Ludwig Spaeth'

'Miss Ellen Willmott'

'Lavendar Lady'

'Charles Joly'

Syringa × persica

'Georges Bellair'

TAXUS SPECIES

TAK-sus

Yew

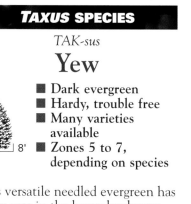

7'
8'

- Dark evergreen
- Hardy, trouble free
- Many varieties available
- Zones 5 to 7, depending on species

This versatile needled evergreen has many uses in the home landscape, but the seeds are toxic, as is the foliage.

USE: Yew is good for formal hedges, massing, topiary, shrub borders, and foundation plantings. Growth rate: slow.

CULTURE: Plant in soil with excellent drainage in sun or shade. In hot, dry climates, place them with a northern exposure. Water in dry sites and protect them from sweeping wind. It may be browsed by deer. The red fruits of the female plants contain highly toxic black seeds.

RECOMMENDED SPECIES:
T. baccata (English yew; zones 6 to 7) is good for southern gardens. 'Adpressa Fowle' (dwarf boxleaf English yew) is a shade-tolerant compact yew, with distinctive short needles, growing 7 feet high and twice as wide. 'Repandens' is a graceful low form for massing, useful in zones 5 to 7. *T. cuspidata* (Japanese yew; zones 4 to 7), has

many excellent cultivars. 'Aurescens' is a dwarf with yellow new growth. 'Densa' is a thick mass of upright stems 2 to 3 feet high and 3 to 4 feet wide. Var. capitata (sometimes sold as 'Capitata') is a botanical variety quite variable from seed. *T. × media* (Anglojap yew; zones 5 to 7) is a hybrid between the previous two species. 'Beanpole' has bright red fruit and stands 3 to 4 feet high and 6 to 8 inches wide. 'Hatfieldii' (Hatfield yew) is a broad, upright hedging plant, 12 feet high and 10 feet wide. 'Hicksii' (Hick's yew) is a good hedging plant with dark green leaves and columnar habit, 6 to 8 feet high and 3 to 4 feet wide.

Taxus baccata *'Repependens Aurea'*

Taxus baccata *'Fastigiata Aureomarginata'*

Taxus baccata *'Fastigiata'*

Taxus cuspidata *'Dwarf Bright'*

A seedling of Taxus cuspidata *var.* capitata

Another seedling of T. cuspidata *var.* capitata; note the variation from the one at left.

Taxus × media *'Hicksii'* makes a good subject for a formal hedge.

The natural form of T. × media *'Hicksii'* is columnar.

Taxus × media *'Densiflora'*

THUJA OCCIDENTALIS

THOO-ya ok-si-den-TAL-is

American arborvitae

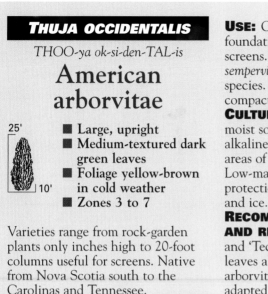

25'
10'

- Large, upright
- Medium-textured dark green leaves
- Foliage yellow-brown in cold weather
- Zones 3 to 7

Varieties range from rock-garden plants only inches high to 20-foot columns useful for screens. Native from Nova Scotia south to the Carolinas and Tennessee.

USE: Cultivars are found in foundation plantings, hedges, and screens. Plant it with *Iberis sempervirens* and *Chamaecyparis* species. Growth rate: slow for compact cultivars.

CULTURE: Plant in well-drained moist soil in full sun. It tolerates alkaline soils and performs best in areas of high atmospheric moisture. Low-maintenance, it needs some protection from winter winds, snow, and ice.

RECOMMENDED CULTIVARS AND RELATED SPECIES: 'Nigra' and 'Techny' retain dark green leaves all winter. *T. plicata* (giant arborvitae) cultivars are better adapted to the central Midwest

than *T. occidentalis*, and are reportedly not as palatable to deer.

'Emerald Giant' is cute when young, but can grow 4 feet a year for a rapid screen. Inset: 'Rhinegold', a dwarf.

TSUGA CANADENSIS 'PENDULA'

SOO-ga kan-a-DEN-sis PEN-dew-la

Sargent's weeping hemlock

8'
15'

- Pendulous habit
- Refined evergreen foliage
- Trouble free in the right location
- Zones 4 to 8 south

This is the most commonly grown dwarf cultivar of this coniferous tree. Native from Nova Scotia to Minnesota and south along the

Appalachians to Alabama and Georgia.

USE: Sargent's weeping hemlock makes an outstanding focal point in the landscape, and also is good for shrub borders and foundation plantings. Use it with *Cryptomeria japonica* 'Yoshino' and *Sciadopitys verticillata*. It can reach a height of 10 feet or more, with a spread of 20 feet, in great old age (50 years or more). Growth rate: slow to moderate.

CULTURE: Plant in well-drained, moist, acid soil in partial shade. It tolerates sun if drainage is good, soil is moist, and there are no dry winds. Do not plant in polluted areas or where temperatures exceed 95° F.

Sargent's weeping hemlock is a slow-growing tree with a mounding, shrublike habit.

VACCINIUM CORYMBOSUM

vak-SIN-i-um ko-rim-BOW-sum

Highbush blueberry

6'
6'

- Colorful fall foliage
- Blue fruit
- Dark purplish red stems
- Zones 5 to 8 north

Primarily grown for its fruit, this is a choice four-season landscape plant that has white flowers and yellow, bronze, orange, or red fall colors. Native from Maine to Minnesota and south to Florida and Louisiana.

USE: Good for shrub borders, foundation plantings, and massed naturally in large areas. Blueberry grows well with *Viburnum trilobum* 'Compactum' and *Ribes* species. Growth rate: slow.

CULTURE: Blueberries do best in sandy, acid soil in full sun, but they also produce in moist, acid, well-drained soil high in organic matter. Mulch well to promote a cool, moist root run and water during drought.

RECOMMENDED CULTIVARS AND RELATED SPECIES: Check with your local cooperative extension for the best cultivars for your locale. *V. angustifolium* (lowbush blueberry; zones 2 to 5) has blue-green leaves and open

habit up to 2 feet high and 2 feet wide. It thrives in poor, thirsty, acid soil, and provides bright red fall color and delectable berries.

Above: The brilliant fall color of lowbush blueberry, V. angustifolium. Inset: Highbush blueberry with fruit.

VIBURNUM SPECIES

vy-bur'-num

Viburnum

- Some are fragrant
- Flowers and fruit
- Evergreen and deciduous species
- Zones 3 to 9, depending on the species

This diverse genus contains a range of valuable shrubs for the garden and some species have fine fall color.

USE: They can be used in shrub borders, in groups, or for massing. They also can be used as landscape specimens or, depending on the species, as bird-attracting shrubs in a wildlife garden. Plant them with *Hydrangea quercifolia* and *Rhus copallina*, and with other viburnums. Growth rate: Moderate.

CULTURE: Plant in moist, well-drained, slightly acid soil, although they're generally adaptable to other soils. If kept vigorous, these shrubs are usually untroubled by pests and diseases.

RECOMMENDED SPECIES:

V. × burkwoodii (Burkwood viburnum; zones 5 to 8) is an upright, somewhat straggly shrub 8 to 10 feet high and 5 to 7 feet wide, grown for its fragrant pink flowers that appear in mid-spring before leaves unfold. Evergreen in the South; semievergreen in the North.

V. × carlcephalum (fragrant snowball viburnum; zones 6 to 9) has loose, open growth 6 to 10 feet high and wide. It produces sweetly fragrant white flowers in April or May.

V. carlesii (Korean spice viburnum; zones 5 to 7) has spicy sweet pinkish-white flowers in late April to early May on a rounded, dense shrub 4 to 8 feet high and 4 to 8 feet wide. Popular in northern gardens. Native to Korea.

V. davidii (David viburnum, zones 8 to 10) is a dense, large-leaved evergreen shrub 1 to 3 feet high and 3 to 4 feet wide with dark metallic blue fruits. Native to China, it grows well in California gardens.

V. dentatum (arrowwood viburnum; zones 4 to 8) is hardy and adaptable to many climates and harsh conditions. It has a dense habit with spreading branches, 6 to 15 feet high and wide, and white flowers and blue-black fruits. Native from New Brunswick south to Florida and Texas.

V. dilatatum (Linden viburnum; Zones 5 to 8) is an upright, open shrub 8 to 10 feet high and 5 to 8 feet wide with white, unpleasant-smelling flowers in May and June. Its most outstanding season is September and October, when the bright red fruits ripen, often remaining effective into December. Plant in shrub borders and grow several together to improve fruiting. Native to eastern Asia.

V. × juddii (Judd viburnum; zones 5 to 7) is similar to *V. carlesii* but taller and more heat tolerant.

V. macrocephalum (Chinese snowball viburnum; zones 7 to 8) bears white, round balls of sterile flowers up to 8 inches across in late May to early June; they are the largest flower clusters of any viburnum. A dense, rounded shrub, it is semievergreen in southern areas and 6 to 10 feet high and wide. In the northern part of its range, it needs protection from winter winds and must have well-drained soil. Native to China.

V. opulus (European cranberrybush; zones 4 to 8) produces delicate white pinwheel flowers, composed of sterile showy flowers on the outside of the cluster and fertile, less conspicuous flowers on the inside, in late May. Bright red berrylike fruits are effective from September to November, accompanied by excellent fall color. It grows 8 to 15 feet tall and 10 to 15 feet wide. Susceptible to aphids, especially the snowball-flowered cultivar 'Roseum'. Native to Europe.

V. plicatum f. tomentosum 'Mariesii' (doublefile viburnum, zones 5 to 8) is often considered the most beautiful of all deciduous flowering shrubs. It bears profuse, lacy, pure white pinwheel flowers gracefully arranged along horizontally tiered branches. It stands 8 to 10 feet high and slightly wider with dark green foliage in summer and good fall color. Bright red fruits in late summer are attractive to birds. Excellent with broad-leaved evergreens, as a focal specimen, for horizontal balance in upright shrub borders, against dark red brick, or with red flowers. It needs fertile, well-drained, moist soil for easy maintenance. 'Mariesii' and 'Shasta' bear the largest flower and fruit clusters. 'Pink Beauty' produces smaller, deep pink flowers, and 'Shasta' has profuse, very large white flowers and exceptional horizontal branching. Native to China and Japan.

V. × rhytidophylloides 'Willow Wood' (Lantanaphyllum viburnum; zones 6 to 7) has large, leathery semievergreen leaves on a shrub that reaches 8 to 10 feet high and wide.

V. setigerum (tea viburnum; zones 5 to 7) is grown for dramatic red fruit display on tall, arching branches. It stands 10 to 12 feet high and up to 8 feet wide. Tea viburnum works well when grown behind shorter shrubs, which cover the bare-bottomed stems responsible for its unusual, top-heavy but striking appearance. Native to China.

V. tinus (Laurustinus; zones 8 to 10) is an evergreen, upright, 6- to 12-foot-high shrub for southern and West Coast gardens. It has dark green foliage, pink flowers turning to white, and bright metallic blue fruit. Dense, groundhugging leaves make it good for screening, and it responds well to formal pruning. Adaptable to shade but flowers more in full sun.

V. trilobum (American cranberrybush viburnum; zones 4 to 8). This is a North American native similar to European cranberrybush but hardier and more resistant to aphids. 'Compactum' is a fine dwarf form with red autumn foliage but few fruits, at least when planted alone.

V. × burkwoodii *'Chenault'*

V. × burkwoodii *'Mohawk'*

V. × carlcephalum

V. × carlcephalum *flowers*

V. carlesii

V. carlesii, *fall color*

V. dentatum

V. davidii

V. dilatatum *'Eric'*

V. dilitatum *'Eric', fruit*

V. opulus *'Roseum'*

V. opulus, *fall color*

V. plicatum tomentosum *'Mariesii'*

V. plicatum tomuntosum *'Shoshoni', flower detail*

V. plicatum tomuntosum *'Shasta', fruit detail*

V. macrocephalum *'Sterile'*

V. setigerum *'Aurantiacum'*

V. tinus *'Robustum'*

V. trilobum *in bloom*

V. trilobum *in fall*

WEIGELA FLORIDA

wye-JEE-la FLOR-i-da

Old-fashioned wiegela

7'
8'

- Flowers in many colors
- Dark green leaves of medium texture
- Coarse and rangy
- Zones 5 to 8, some cultivars in colder zones

The floral display in late May and early June is outstanding. Some new forms, such as 'Wine and Roses', have good foliage. Native to northern China and Korea.

USE: Plant in the shrub border, in masses, and in groupings, where its form and texture can be hidden when not flowering. Combine wiegela with *Abelia* × *grandiflora* and *Fothergilla gardenii*. Growth rate: Moderate.

CULTURE: Prefers well-drained soil and a sunny location but is adaptable and pest-free. Prune after flowering to clean up the shrub's appearance.

RECOMMENDED CULTIVARS: Var. *venusta* is hardy to zone 4 with finely textured leaves and rosy pink flowers. 'Bristol Ruby', 'Red Prince', and 'Vaniceki' have red flowers. 'Red Prince' is the most cold hardy of these. 'Minuet' is low growing, to 3 feet tall, with reddish purple foliage and pink flowers, cold hardy to at least zone 3.

Weigela florida *'Aurea'*

Weigela florida *'Pink Princess'*

Weigela florida *'Variegata'*

YUCCA FILAMENTOSA

YUK-ka fil-a-men-TOH-sa

Adam's needle

6'
3'

- Leaves to 3 feet long
- Bell-shaped flowers
- Leaves radiate around the stalk
- Zones 5 to 9

Striking architectural plant has narrow, stiff, arched, sword-like evergreen leaves and white flowers on a stout central stalk 3 to 8 feet high. Native to the southeastern United States.

USE: Plant it in shrub borders, containers, desert gardens, or massed as a ground cover. It combines well with *Tamarix hispida* and *Rosemarinus officinalis*. It also makes an excellent specimen in the landscape. Growth rate: Slow.

CULTURE: Adam's needle grows well in the hot, humid climate of the Gulf States, in the desert, and in average well-drained garden soil. It needs excellent drainage. It does better in full sun and poor soils low in organic matter, but can adapt to many soils and partial shade. Drought tolerant.

RECOMMENDED CULTIVARS AND RELATED SPECIES: 'Golden Sword' has leaves with green edges and yellow centers. 'Variegata' has cream-striped foliage. 'Bright Edge' has leaves with cream edges and green centers. *Y. glauca* (soapweed; Zones 4 to 10) is a hardy midwestern native. It has leaves about 1 inch wide and 2 to 3 feet long with gray green centers and lighter edges. A central stalk 3 feet long bears greenish white flowers.

'Golden Sword' is a variegated form of Adam's needle.

The flower spikes on Yucca filamentosa *can reach 8 feet high.*

INDEX

Pages numbers in italics denote photographs. Boldface numbers refer to lead entries in the "Selection and Growing Guide."

MAIL ORDER SOURCES

Carroll Gardens
444 E. Main St.
Westminster, MD 21157
800-638-6334
Deciduous flowering shrubs

Dilworth Nursery
1200 Election Road
Oxford, PA 19363
610-932-0347
Dwarf and unusual

Eastern Plant Specialties
P.O. Box 226
Georgetown, ME 04548
207-371-2888
*Hardy rhododendrons and azaleas,
dwarf conifers, hollies, kalmias,
pieris, and other unusual shrubs*

Gossler Farms Nursery
1200 Weaver Road
Springfield, OR 97478-3922
541-746-6611
General

Greer Gardens
1280 Goodpasture Island Road
Eugene, OR 97401-1794

541-686-8266
*Rhododendrons, azaleas, conifers,
hydrangeas, and other selected
shrubs*

Heard Gardens, Ltd.
5355 Merle Hay Road
Johnston, IA 50131
515-276-4533
Lilacs

Heirloom Old Garden Roses
24062 NE Riverside Dr.
St. Paul, OR 97137
503-538-1576
Own root, old garden roses

Roslyn Nursery
211 Burrs Lane
Dix Hills, NY 11746
516-643-9347
*Wide selection of rhododendrons,
azaleas, conifers (incl. dwarf),
buddleias, clethra, enkianthus,
hamamelis, fothergilla, hydrangeas,
itea, viburnums*

Siskiyou Rare Plant Nursery
2825 Cummings Road

Medford, OR 97501-1538
541-772-6846
*Wide selection of dwarf unusual
shrubs, including conifers, daphnes,
heaths and heathers*

Wayside Gardens
P.O. Box 1
Hodges, SC 29695-0001
800-845-1124
General

White Flower Farm
P.O. Box 50
Litchfield, CT 06759-0050
800-503-9624
Garden roses, selected shrubs

Woodlanders
1128 Colleton Ave.
Aiken, SC 29801
803-648-7522
Rare and hard-to-find shrubs

Yucca Do Nursery
P.O. Box 5104
Hempstead, TX 77445
409-826-4580
Shrubs and plants for the Southwest

METRIC CONVERSIONS

U.S. Units to Metric Equivalents			Metric Units to U.S. Equivalents		
To Convert From	Multiply By	To Get	To Convert From	Multiply By	To Get
Inches	25.4	Millimeters	Millimeters	0.0394	Inches
Inches	2.54	Centimeters	Centimeters	0.3937	Inches
Feet	30.48	Centimeters	Centimeters	0.0328	Feet
Feet	0.3048	Meters	Meters	3.2808	Feet
Yards	0.9144	Meters	Meters	1.0936	Yards
Square inches	6.4516	Square centimeters	Square centimeters	0.1550	Square inches
Square feet	0.0929	Square meters	Square meters	10.764	Square feet
Square yards	0.8361	Square meters	Square meters	1.1960	Square yards
Acres	0.4047	Hectares	Hectares	2.4711	Acres
Cubic inches	16.387	Cubic centimeters	Cubic centimeters	0.0610	Cubic inches
Cubic feet	0.0283	Cubic meters	Cubic meters	35.315	Cubic feet
Cubic feet	28.316	Liters	Liters	0.0353	Cubic feet
Cubic yards	0.7646	Cubic meters	Cubic meters	1.308	Cubic yards
Cubic yards	764.55	Liters	Liters	0.0013	Cubic yards

To convert from degrees Fahrenheit (F) to degrees Celsius (C), first subtract 32, then multiply by $\frac{5}{9}$.

To convert from degrees Celsius to degrees Fahrenheit, multiply by $\frac{9}{5}$, then add 32.